Worthy
by
Design

Worthy
by
Design

A NERVOUS SYSTEM GUIDE
TO HEALING, SELF-WORTH,
AND DESIGNING A
LIFE YOU LOVE

JANET BROWN

WHITE RAVEN PRESS

Worthy by Design
A Nervous System Guide to Healing, Self-Worth,
and Designing a Life You Love

Published by White Raven Press
York, Maine

First Edition

ISBN: 979-8-9958433-0-6 (paperback) ISBN: 979-8-9958433-1-3 (e-book)

Library of Congress Control Number 2026910654

Cover and Interior Design by Ian Koviak

Printed in the United States of America

For my husband — my steady ground

And for my children — may you always know your worth

CONTENTS

INTRODUCTION

There was a time when I believed I needed to fix myself to feel whole, and that healing meant repairing every wound until I finally became someone worthy. For years, I approached healing as a project: something to work on, fix, or perfect. I thought wholeness lived somewhere on the other side of achieving or proving myself. But the deeper I went, the more I realized that I was never broken; my body was just adapting and surviving. The truth I found is that healing begins not with fixing, but with remembering our inherent worth.

This book emerged from the moment I stopped trying to become a different version of myself and started listening to the version that had been here all along. As I learned to understand my nervous system, its signals, stories, and survival strategies, I began to see that healing was not about striving toward worthiness but coming home to it.

For me, healing came quietly at first, then began to unfold with momentum. I experienced more moments of reflection, and deep, meaningful conversations. As I made progress, I felt inspired and hopeful that my experiences could help others find their own path to nervous system healing. Reconnecting with myself brought a sense of joy, peace, and purpose I hadn't known before, and I knew I had to share what I was learning.

Along the way, I discovered that the abundance I had been chasing wasn't eluding me because I was broken, or because I was saying the wrong affirmations, or visualizing incorrectly. The truth was simpler and more profound: There were steps missing in the way abundance is often taught. Every dream I had—success, peace, rest, a sense of being enough—rested on one foundation: nervous system wealth.

This book may have found its way to you for many reasons: You might feel exhausted but unable to rest. You may be burned out, chasing your worth through performance, or afraid to step out of the shadows with your gifts. Perhaps you've tried mindset tools or abundance practices that didn't work or felt hollow. We'll explore all of this and more—together.

What you hold in your hands is a guide back to yourself. In these pages, we move slowly and intentionally, from understanding the body's responses, to meeting ourselves with compassion, to designing a life that reflects who we truly are.

Each chapter builds upon the last, creating a steady path from survival to safety, from safety to self-worth, and from self-worth to conscious design. We return to the body again and again until safety becomes familiar, until compassion becomes instinctual, and until worthiness becomes the ground we walk on.

This book serves as both a map and a mirror. It will illuminate the parts of yourself you've been avoiding while guiding you toward the life you want to live. Together, we will walk with your shadow and gently trace the roots of generational conditioning and inherited beliefs. We will explore emotional patterns, triggers, and self-worth wounds—all through the lens of compassion. Along the way, you'll plant new roots of safety: boundaries, self-respect, presence, and gratitude. Step by step, the path leads you back to wholeness, safety, and alignment.

This book is for anyone who has ever confused busyness with safety, or self-worth with self-sacrifice. It is for those who have spent years trying to earn what was already theirs—the feeling of being enough. It is an invitation to remember your value, to rest, to heal, and to reconnect with the wisdom already within you.

Here, you will root in safety, rise in self-trust, and design a life that is aligned and worthy. My hope is that as you move through these chapters, you feel yourself exhaling, and that you remember your worth, not as something to chase, but as something that has always belonged to you.

HOW TO USE THIS BOOK

We live in a world that teaches us to rise before we root, to perform without pausing, and to measure our worth by what we produce and accumulate. When we try to grow without first establishing safety, our nervous system can remain on alert, leaving us exhausted, disconnected, and unsure of our inherent value. This book is an invitation to rebuild your foundation of safety and self-worth so that you can blossom into who you were always meant to be.

The book is divided into three parts:

- **Root:** This part helps you gain a stronger understanding of how your body stores trauma, memories, and experiences. We explore how this shapes the lens through which you see the world. This is where safety begins—with awareness.
- **Rise:** We explore how to rewire emotional loops and set boundaries. This is how we shift out of survival mode, by using practices such as presence and gratitude.
- **Design:** We integrate growth through alignment, expression, and abundance. This is the embodiment of nervous system wealth.

Keep in mind that there is no right or wrong way to move through this book. You might choose to read it cover to cover, and then return to it later. Or you may prefer to take it one chapter at a time, pausing to complete the journal prompts and nervous system reset practices as you go. You can even open it at random and see what page calls to you. Perhaps that moment of synchronicity will point you toward what your body and heart need most that day.

Each chapter includes:

- **Core Teaching:** the central concept of the chapter
- **A Nervous System Reset:** grounding practices that regulate and restore safety
- **Journal Prompts:** guided questions to help integrate your learning
- **Rewiring Your Outlook:** simple affirmations and mantras that embody the chapter's core theme
- **Going Forward:** closing reflections and next steps

Some of the reflections and journal prompts may bring up strong memories or emotions. If a section feels overwhelming, take a pause. Step away, breathe, and come back when you feel ready. Healing moves at the pace of safety. And if a topic feels too heavy to navigate alone, reach out for support or simply talk it through with someone you trust.

Be Gentle with Yourself

Move at your own pace. Pause when you need to. Wherever you are right now is perfectly okay. There is no rush, no race, no finish line in healing. Growth is a lifelong process, a spiral rather than a straight line, and even small moments of awareness create profound change over time.

REMEMBER: Move at the pace of your body. If you feel overwhelmed or need support, consider reaching out to a licensed mental healthcare professional or a trusted healthcare provider.

By picking up this book, you've already taken an important step. Simply having the awareness that things could feel better means you're ready to learn, ready to heal, and ready to meet yourself with more compassion than before.

What Is Nervous System Wealth?

Nervous system wealth is the experience of inner safety that allows you to access your intuition, alignment, and natural creativity. It is the deep knowing that you are enough, just as you are.

When your nervous system feels safe enough to receive, you will find that success, love, and authentic expression flow naturally. You cannot create abundance from a place of contraction. You cannot rise and expand until you are rooted in safety.

Somatic Moments & Self-Care

A somatic moment is a body-based experience of awareness and reconnection. It invites you to be present with your body and notice sensations, emotions, or tension with gentle curiosity. For example, taking a slow breath and feeling your chest rise and fall.

There is a subtle, but important, distinction between somatic moments and self-care. Self-care is a broader practice of caring for your mind and body. It supports your physical, emotional, and energetic well-being through intentional actions such as taking a bath, journaling, or preparing nourishing food. Somatic moments and self-care beautifully complement each other.

The nervous system reset may weave somatic moments and self-care together, and include a simple, embodied sequence designed to help you integrate what you've learned. These practices are designed to help you return to grounded presence and have a felt sense of safety. Integrating these practices into daily life allows you to expand your capacity for regulation, connection, and healing.

The journal prompts in each chapter are grouped into: Notice, Reflect, and Integrate. You may move though them in order, or you might choose what feels most supportive in the moment.

Affirmations & Mantras

The Rewiring Your Outlook section includes a simple affirmation or mantra, which is an intentional use of language to help shift your inner state. An affirmation is a conscious statement of truth or intention, designed to reprogram limiting beliefs and create new thought patterns that support your healing, self-worth, and capacity to welcome abundance.

Mantras, while similar, have slightly different roots. Traditionally, a mantra is a vibrational practice, where a sound or phrase is repeated to focus the mind and steady the energy of the body. In modern use, a mantra can simply be any phrase that helps you ground, return to presence, and reconnect with your center.

As you move into the first chapter, I invite you to take your time and let these pages meet you exactly where you are. This book is not something to get through; it is something to move with. My hope is that each chapter becomes an opening, guiding you gently back to yourself. When you're ready, turn the page. Your journey into nervous system wealth begins now.

ROOT

Reclaiming Safety & Self-Compassion

—

THE MYTH OF BROKENNESS

Her exhaustion seeped deep into her bones. She was caught in an endless loop of trying to be better, to fix, to improve, all the while placing unrealistic expectations on herself. Each attempt was followed by what she saw as failure, then disappointment, then shame.

She stood in front of the mirror, hardly able to meet her own eyes as waves of self-criticism washed over her. Then the familiar story loops began:

> *Why can't I have the perfect body everyone else seems to have without effort?*
>
> *I look awful in these clothes. I need to change. Maybe I should just stay home. It's not like anyone would care if I went or not.*
>
> *Why aren't I further along in life? I should have saved more money by now. Everyone else my age seems successful. What did I do wrong? Maybe I just don't deserve it.*
>
> *If I were better, maybe things would have turned out differently.*

Does any of this sound familiar? If it does, you are not alone. These inner monologues are heartbreakingly common. We've been conditioned to become our own worst critics instead of our biggest supporters. Staring at our reflection, we judge, we criticize, we tear ourselves down. But why?

Years of societal and generational conditioning have convinced us that we are not enough, don't have enough, and will never be enough. A small voice whispers that we do not have love, happiness, or success in our lives because we have not earned it, or that we do not deserve it, or that we are unworthy of it.

But what if we could believe that our worthiness isn't something to prove or perfect? What if we could remember that we are worthy simply by being ourselves, flaws and all? *Worthy by design.*

The feeling of being broken or unworthy is familiar to many, especially to those carrying trauma, sensitivity, or the weight of societal pressure. We haven't yet realized that this is a myth, which over time embeds itself into the nervous system, shaping how we see ourselves and respond to the world.

Societal norms can compound these issues. We have been taught that struggle equals failure and that only perfection is to be rewarded. We scroll through curated glimpses of other lives and compare our day-to-day moments to highlight reels. *Look how happy she looks . . . look at that vacation . . . what a perfect life.* And then we turn inward and blame ourselves for falling short. Shame takes root. It hides in the body, feeding looping narratives of self-doubt and unworthiness: *I am not enough. I am not worthy.*

Understanding Shame & the Body

While guilt is connected to what we do, shame becomes entwined with who we believe we are. It seeps into identity and tells us that we are unworthy. This belief then becomes the foundation upon which we feel, relate, and make decisions.

Internalized shame reflects the core belief that something is inherently wrong with you. It often grows from moments of emotional neglect or invalidation, from unmet needs, conditional love, or cultural and religious messages that tell us we are "less than." In response, we develop habits that keep our nervous system feeling safe while carrying that hidden shame.

Recognizing the Patterns

Many common behaviors and feelings that are misread as personal flaws are, in fact, intelligent nervous system coping strategies. You may recognize yourself in one or many of the following:

Internal States

- Feeling guilty for relaxing or resting
- A baseline sense of tension, urgency, or anxiety
- Difficulty feeling safe in stillness or silence
- Chronic self-doubt
- Feeling behind in life, fueling a constant need to do more
- Fear of being seen, heard, or taking up space
- Feeling undeserving of ease, success, or support
- Shame that arises without a clear cause
- Feeling like "too much" or "not enough"

Behavior Patterns

- People-pleasing or chronic self-monitoring
- Overthinking, procrastinating, or freezing before action
- Pushing toward perfectionism to avoid criticism or rejection
- Withdrawing when overwhelmed
- Overworking or staying busy to avoid feeling
- Avoiding conflict even at personal cost
- Seeking external validation
- Oscillating between over-functioning and collapse

Beneath these patterns, there is often a quiet story unfolding within. It may whisper: *There must be something wrong with me. Other people can handle this so why can't I? It's safer not to want too much. If I were truly worthy, this would be easier.*

These narratives tend to surface in moments of stillness or vulnerability. They can feel convincing, but they are protective echoes of past nervous system responses. They are not a reflection of who you are.

None of these are evidence that you are broken. They are survival responses. Your body has tried to keep you safe, but in doing so, it may have limited your capacity to rest, grow, receive, and rise.

Reframing Survival as Wisdom

Our nervous system is not flawed. It is doing exactly what it was designed to do: protect us. Sometimes that protection looks like the patterns mentioned previously, but these are safety strategies, not your identity.

When you view these responses with compassion rather than shame, you loosen the old narrative of brokenness. Shame can be intensely damaging to our sense of self-worth, and that relationship with ourselves must be healed before we can blossom. Shame may have kept you small, but awareness offers freedom. What you once called flaws are really just messages from your body, inviting you to listen instead of judge. Finding grace toward yourself is the beginning of true change. You are not broken, and your worth does not need to be earned. It only needs to be remembered.

Nervous System Reset: Small Gestures for Yourself

As we move through this book, the Nervous System Resets gradually guide you into deeper layers of self-care. For this first chapter, we simply dip a toe into small, accessible practices that signal safety to the body.

You may already do some of these practices, and that is wonderful. If not, that is perfectly okay, too. We start small because, when the nervous system is dysregulated, even positive experiences like getting a massage can feel overwhelming if they are too much or too big of a shift. Safety grows through gentle, consistent acts of care, one small moment at a time.

Each new pathway represents a stage of capacity, the first being intentionally gentle and low stakes, helping you build a foundation of basic safety and self-nourishment. Choose the practices that feel possible and supportive today.

The Practice

Regulate the Body

- Stay hydrated throughout the day.

- Sit down while you eat; avoid rushing or multitasking. Savor each bite.

- Incorporate gentle daily movement, even five minutes of stretching or walking.

- Wear something cozy and comfortable, as comfort signals safety to the body.

- Soften your face and shoulders; unclench your jaw.

Protect Rest & Recovery

- Prioritize sleep. Keep consistent bed and wake times.

- Make your sleep environment peaceful and conducive to rest.

- Take a few deep breaths before getting out of bed.

Create Micro-Moments of Safety

- Turn off phone notifications for a few minutes to enjoy uninterrupted time.

- Spend a few minutes in nature. If that's not possible, look at photos of calming landscapes.

- Enjoy a cup of coffee or tea without distractions.

- When you catch yourself saying something negative about yourself, pause and stop the comment mid-thought.

These small gestures may seem simple, but they are powerful. They teach your body that it is safe to slow down, to receive, and to care for itself, one gentle step at a time.

Journal Prompts

Notice

- Were there any moments of relief or recognition as you read? Did you feel anything that shifted, even subtly?

- As you reflect on this chapter, what sensations, emotions, or images do you notice in your body, without trying to change them? What feels most tender or protected inside you right now?

- What parts of you have been trying very hard to get things "right"?

Reflect

- What behaviors, patterns, or traits have you often judged in yourself as character flaws? How might they have once served a protective purpose?

- Can you remember a time when you believed something was wrong with you? How does it feel to question that belief now?

- What expectations have you placed on yourself that now feel heavy, unrealistic, or unkind?

Integrate

- How would you treat yourself differently if you truly believed you were not broken?

- What would it feel like to stop measuring yourself, even briefly?

Rewiring Your Outlook

Worthiness lives within me.

Going Forward

As you move forward from this chapter, notice the moments when your inner dialogue turns toward judgment or self-doubt. Pause and take a breath. Ask yourself: *What is my body trying to protect me from right now?*

Awareness is the first step toward change. When you see your patterns as protection rather than proof of failure, you open the door to compassion. Over time, that compassion becomes the bridge that leads you out of survival mode and into trust, rest, and genuine self-worth. Healing doesn't require fixing what is "wrong" with you. It begins with remembering that nothing about you was ever broken.

In the next chapter, we will give shape to what you have begun uncovering here. If the myth of brokenness was the veil, your nervous system is the compass beneath it, the guide that has been speaking to you all along. We will explore how your nervous system works, why it responds the way it does, and how to recognize its patterns without fear or judgment. Understanding this inner compass is the foundation of every transformation that follows.

—

CHAPTER 2

NERVOUS SYSTEM 101
Your Inner Compass

Your nervous system is your inner compass at work. It is constantly scanning for cues of danger and cues of safety. For instance, when you walk into a room, before anything has even happened, your body subtly reacts based on what it remembers about similar rooms.

Within the autonomic nervous system, the part of the body that manages involuntary functions such as heartbeat, breathing, and digestion, there are two main branches. The sympathetic state governs our fight-or-flight response to stress, while the parasympathetic state supports rest and digest functions that allow us to recover and restore balance.

According to Polyvagal Theory, developed by Dr. Stephen Porges, there is a third response within this system: the dorsal vagal state, also known as collapse or freeze. This is the immobilization response that occurs when fight or flight feels impossible. We naturally move through all three states throughout the day. The goal isn't to remain perfectly regulated at all times, or always in a state of rest and digest, but to be able to return to regulation when we leave it, an ability known as flexibility of the nervous system.

One of the major components of the parasympathetic system is the vagus nerve. When it functions properly, it signals safety to the body and helps us return to a state of calm after stress. When the nervous system becomes dysregulated, vagal tone weakens, and the body can remain stuck in fight, flight, or freeze states. Over time, this can contribute to a variety of physical and emotional symptoms.

Many of us live in this dysregulated state, an imbalance between the sympathetic and parasympathetic systems. This can feel like being perpetually on edge, waiting for the other shoe to drop, or conversely, like being numb and shut down. When we push ourselves for too long, relaxation itself can feel foreign or unsafe. I personally pushed my body through years of sleep deprivation, unprocessed trauma, and stress until it felt as if my system had forgotten how to rest. My body had learned to equate stillness with danger.

Dysregulation often results from trauma, chronic stress, or emotions that have never been fully processed. But your nervous system is not broken. It is protecting you in the only way it knows how, even if that means keeping you small, quiet, or constantly on high alert.

Chronic Stress & the Nervous System

Bursts of stress are not inherently bad and are sometimes the result of positive experiences like exercise. They can even be motivating in short doses. But when the body stays in an activated state for extended periods, stress becomes chronic. Stress hormones remain elevated, and the body loses access to rest and repair. Over time, this drains energy, erodes resilience, and may contribute to physical, mental, and emotional symptoms.

Cortisol & Adrenaline in the Body

When stress arises, the body releases the hormones cortisol and adrenaline. These hormones are essential for mobilizing energy and helping us respond to danger, but problems can occur when they stay elevated for too long. The body becomes stuck in overdrive, unable to relax or feel safe.

We need access to the upper parts of our brain to make thoughtful and intentional decisions, and have access to empathy, perspective, understanding, and emotional regulation—but that access depends on a sense of safety in the body. When our body is in a state of stress response, the nervous system redirects resources away from these higher states of thinking and toward survival. This is a protective response, and our capacity to pause, reflect, and respond with care naturally narrows until the body returns to a state of safety.

Your Stress Chemistry & the HPA Axis

The HPA axis—short for the hypothalamic-pituitary-adrenal axis—is the communication loop between your brain and your adrenal glands. This system activates when your body senses danger, physical or emotional, releasing stress hormones such as cortisol and adrenaline. This stress response prepares you to protect yourself.

This is helpful during true emergencies, but when your life has held long stretches of stress, overwhelm, or high pressure, the HPA axis can stay switched on. When that happens, you may experience some of the following:

- You feel wired but tired.
- Rest doesn't feel restorative.
- You have racing thoughts.

- Presence feels difficult.
- Happiness feels out of reach.
- Your body interprets normal life as danger.

This is why healing your nervous system matters so deeply. As you regulate your system and relearn safety, the HPA axis softens, your cortisol lowers, and your body is again able to experience joy, gratitude, and grounded presence.

Your Nervous System State Matters More Than Mindset

The state you are in shapes the story you tell yourself. When your nervous system is regulated, life feels manageable and full of possibility. When it is dysregulated, everything can feel heavy, threatening, or out of reach. Your body's reactions are not signs of weakness; they are survival strategies learned over time.

The healing path is not about forcing your mind to think positively, but about helping your body remember what safety feels like. We can show our bodies how to feel safe in situations that might have caused a nervous system reaction in the past. We can teach the body to find safety in new ways that do not require us to overperform, withdraw, or abandon ourselves. When we show the body that peace and calm are safe to inhabit, we can shift our story.

Cortisol Clues & Releasing Exercises

You may already recognize some of the classic signs of excess cortisol in the body: poor sleep, persistent fatigue, weight gain, muscle tension, headaches, anxiety, digestive issues, sugar or salt cravings, lowered immunity, brain fog, or a decreased libido. There are also lesser-known signs worth noticing, your body's quiet ways of asking for support. These include:

- Puffy eyes or dark circles: often linked to impaired lymphatic flow and fluid retention from chronic stress

- Jaw clenching or teeth grinding: the body bracing under a perceived threat

- Cold hands and feet: restricted circulation as blood flow is redirected toward survival systems

- Thinning hair or hair shedding: disrupted hair growth cycles from hormonal imbalance

- Skin changes: breakouts, dryness, or inflammation tied to cortisol-driven shifts

- Increased startle response: a sign of heightened alertness

- Restless legs: energy attempting to move through the body

- Bloating or water retention: cortisol's impact on sodium levels and digestion

- Perfectionism: the mind's attempt to regain a sense of safety through control

If you notice any of these signs, your body may be signaling that it's time to complete a stress cycle. Of course, these sensations can also result from other health conditions, so always consult your healthcare provider if you have concerns. The more you learn to listen to your body, the more quickly you can help it return to balance.

Fortunately, there are simple, accessible ways to help release excess cortisol and restore calm to your system. Try experimenting with a few of the following:

- Shaking: allows the body to discharge built-up stress energy through a quick physical reset

- Deep sighing and exhaling audibly: calms the vagus nerve and releases tension

- Intentional yawning: promotes oxygen flow and supports nervous system regulation

- Gentle movement (e.g., walk, stretch, dance, yoga): helps metabolize stress hormones

- Crying: releases emotional tension and allows the body to soften after stress

- Gentle self-massage around the jaw, armpits, and collarbone: supports lymphatic flow and physical relaxation

- Time in nature (even just a few minutes): allows the nervous system to settle and reduces cortisol levels

- Limiting caffeine, screen time, and high-adrenaline environments: reduces overstimulation and supports rest

- Protecting your rest with consistent, adequate sleep patterns: helps regulate cortisol rhythms and supports recovery

- A restorative pose (e.g., child's pose): promotes relaxation

Each of these small, body-based actions remind your nervous system that the threat has passed and that it is safe to return to rest, recovery, and balance.

Nervous System Reset: Vagus Nerve Activation

In this chapter, we learned that the vagus nerve serves as the main communication pathway between the body and the mind. When your vagal tone is strong, you tend to feel grounded, digestion flows smoothly, your heart rate steadies, and you recover from stress more easily.

When vagal tone is low, the opposite happens. You may feel anxious, flat, or stuck in a freeze state. Digestion, sleep, and relaxation feel harder, and even small stressors can feel overwhelming.

The Practice

The good news is that vagal tone can be improved with simple, consistent practices that signal safety to the body. Try incorporating a few of these gentle exercises:

- Slow, deep breathing: Inhale for a count of four and exhale for eight. Long exhales cue the body to relax.

- Humming or chanting: The vibration in your throat sends soothing feedback to the brain and lowers your heart rate.

- Cold exposure: Splash cold water on your face or briefly finish your shower with cool water to stimulate vagal response.

- Gargling: This stimulates the muscles in the throat and soft palate connected to the vagus nerve.

- Gentle neck and shoulder rolling: This is an easy way to release tightness where the vagus nerve travels down the neck.

- Laughter and smiling: The movement of the face and diaphragm during laughter activates vagal pathways.

- Gentle ear or neck massage: A light massage of the area behind your ears and along the side of your neck can help to calm the system.

Journal Prompts

Notice

- When you are under stress, what patterns do you notice in your thoughts and emotions? Do you tend to have the same emotional responses? How does your body feel in those moments?

- How does your body signal that it is moving into a stress response? For instance, do you feel tension, fatigue, or restlessness, or experience shortness of breath?

- Are there people or situations that reliably send you into a state of nervous system dysregulation?

Reflect

- Are there areas in your life where stress feels ongoing or cyclical rather than situational? What might it look like to step out of that cycle?

- Do you feel that you spend more time in a state of regulation or dysregulation? If more often dysregulated, can you recall when that pattern began?

- When you imagine treating your nervous system as a guide rather than a problem to fix, what changes in your body or thoughts?

Integrate

- When your nervous system is tense or stressed, how easy is it for you to shift back toward calm and regulation?

- When do you feel most regulated or grounded during the day, even briefly?

Rewiring Your Outlook

My body is my teacher.

Going Forward

As you move forward, notice how your body communicates with you throughout the day. You may catch yourself holding your breath during stress, taking shallow breaths, or not fully exhaling. This growing awareness can become a gentle reminder from your body that safety can be restored moment by moment.

Building a regulated nervous system begins with small acts repeated over time. Each breath, each pause, each moment of presence and stillness teaches your body that it is safe to relax and receive again.

As you deepen awareness of your body's signals, you may notice patterns that feel familiar yet not entirely your own.

In the next chapter, we explore the stories, survival strategies, and emotional blueprints passed down through families and culture. Understanding these inherited layers is not about blame; it's about liberation. When you can name the conditioning that shaped you, you can finally choose what will continue forward and what will end with you.

—

CHAPTER 3

CONDITIONING, INHERITED BELIEFS & GENERATIONAL HEALING

We are all products of our environment. You did not come into this world with predetermined thoughts or ideas. From an early age, before you could even walk or talk, you were absorbing. You learned how to behave, how to communicate, and what was expected of you. You observed the words and behaviors of those around you, and your personal stories and narratives began to form. As adults, the way we carry ourselves and interact with the world is largely shaped by those early experiences.

We adapted to cultural norms as a means of survival, even when that meant silencing or ignoring our truth. In school, we learned to comply with socially acceptable behavior to avoid rejection or ridicule. We blended into the crowd, careful not to make waves. Over time, that desire to fit in slowly eroded our connection to our authentic self.

This social compliance was often reinforced by our parents, who viewed it as part of "growing up." Painful experiences with peers were considered normal, something everyone had to navigate. Fitting in often felt far more important than expressing who we truly were, with many of our choices shaped by subtle expectations. You might have been praised for being mature as a child, and it felt good to be seen as responsible, but often that maturity was a form of emotional suppression developed to feel safe. Or maybe you had to act as a caregiver for a younger sibling, thus becoming emotionally mature far beyond your years.

Family dynamics also may have pulled us into these roles designed for survival. Maybe you genuinely enjoyed doing homework, or perhaps you were fulfilling the role of "the good kid," because staying out of trouble felt safe and it earned approval. Maybe you became "the good kid" to offset a sibling's behavior, or you received more love by mirroring the traits your caregivers valued. Perhaps one sibling was the troublemaker, and so you became the peacekeeper, trying to diffuse conflict before it boiled over.

Often, these adaptations were born from necessity. If both parents worked long hours, you may have had no choice but to step up and help with a younger sibling. But even when the reasons were practical, the roles still shaped the stories you carried about who you needed to be. Over-functioning and over-performing are often trauma responses, especially when we associate them with praise. If we were rewarded for being helpful or capable, we may now push through exhaustion and ignore our needs in pursuit of that same conditional love.

Inherited Beliefs

What we inherit from our family goes deeper than genetic traits, mannerisms, and traditions. We also inherit beliefs about love, safety, worthiness, and what it means to survive. We are taught how to express or repress emotions, how to interpret scarcity, and how to perceive work and success. These inherited messages often sound like:

- *Emotions are a sign of weakness.*
- *Love must be earned.*
- *People can't be trusted.*
- *You have to work hard for everything.*
- *Life is a struggle.*
- *Rich people are bad.*

As children, we absorb these ideas without question because belonging to our family feels synonymous with survival. We look up to the adults in our lives and learn what is "true" through their lens of experience.

We have also inherited nervous systems shaped by the experiences of our ancestors. Some of those experiences were collective cultural experiences such as war, poverty, economic depressions, and famines. Other experiences were more personal, such as abuse, neglect, or emotional absence. Your mother's silence or your father's anxiety may have been nervous system adaptations to the environments they grew up in. Many of us were taught that crying or resting were signs of weakness. For some, these beliefs may have been compounded by religious or cultural messages that whispered: *You are a sinner. You are bad. You are unworthy. You are impure.*

Shame can also be inherited, creeping silently into the body, passed along through generations. We may have watched our parents or grandparents shrink, stay quiet, or carry exhaustion as proof of virtue. Rest was seen as indulgent or lazy, especially for those who lived through times of extreme hardship. These patterns will continue until we stop and ask: *Where does this belief come from? Does it belong to me? Do I want to rewrite this chapter?*

Generational Trauma Loops

Generational trauma loops are cycles of beliefs, behaviors, and nervous system responses passed down through families. Often unconscious, they continue until someone decides to break them. When a parent says, "That's just how it was when I was a kid," they may not realize they are repeating a cycle that could be broken. The manifestations of how the trauma loops appear may shift, but the energetic imprint remains. Here are some examples of how different trauma loops can move through generations:

A Poverty or Scarcity Loop

A grandparent grows up during the Great Depression, suffering from extreme poverty and scarcity. Their early life experience teaches them that there is never enough, and they internalize that belief. Their child learns about money through that lens and so is hypervigilant about money, saving obsessively, and overworking to avoid the same fate of poverty and scarcity. The grandchild, though not raised in poverty, still inherits the anxiety around money and feels guilty for desiring abundance.

An Emotional Suppression Loop

A parent punished their child's emotional expression, saying things like, "Stop crying or I'll give you something to cry about." That child learns to suppress feelings to stay safe. As an adult, it is a struggle to connect with their own emotions and so unconsciously teach their children, the third generation, that emotions are unsafe.

A Martyr Loop

A mother sacrifices everything for her family, modeling love as self-sacrifice. Her daughter grows up equating love with self-sacrifice and so becomes a people-pleaser who eventually burns out under the weight of everyone else's needs. The granddaughter inherits the same martyr role but also harbors feelings of resentment.

Breaking these loops begins with awareness. You recognize it, have compassion for it, and choose to step onto a new path.

Generational Healing

When I became a parent, I could finally look back and see that my own parents were doing the best they could with what they had. They were caught within their own generational patterns and may not have recognized them. That realization softened something in me.

Generational healing begins when we realize that many of our thoughts, beliefs, and emotional reactions are not our own, they were inherited. When we notice and name them, we can ask: *Is this mine? Where did this come from? What would I choose instead?*

The generational trauma that lives within us will continue to echo forward unless we choose to interrupt the cycle. Awareness is the first act of healing. When we consciously choose to end old cycles, we create space for a new kind of inheritance: one rooted in safety, presence, and love. Breaking generational patterns is one of the most courageous things we can do. It changes our lives, and it also changes the trajectory of humanity itself. As we raise children or mentor others from this grounded place, we plant seeds of regulation and resilience for future generations.

It takes immense courage to go against the grain and do something different from what is expected by family or society. Yet each subtle change—setting new boundaries, expressing hidden emotions, allowing rest without guilt—heals not only your nervous system but your lineage. You are creating a new path for those who will walk after you.

We stand in the middle of generations, those who came before us and those who will come after. We can offer healing to our ancestors and peace to our descendants by ending the trauma cycles and rewriting our stories.

When you sit with what arises, feel it, and release it, you soften the inherited voices of fear and criticism. You step into your own voice, one of compassion and presence. You are not betraying your ancestors by healing; you are honoring them. They are cheering you on.

We are here, in part, to break the cycles of generational trauma, to step out of the cycle and begin a new path. Imagine the ripple effect of this embodied healing extending far beyond your lifetime.

Nervous System Reset: Offer a Small Act of Kindness

When we become caught in cycles of conditioning, generational trauma, or limiting beliefs, the body prioritizes self-preservation over connection. The nervous system becomes guarded, and we may feel isolated or disconnected from others.

A simple, genuine act of kindness, offered freely, without the expectation of receiving anything in return, can help retrain the body to feel safe in connection. Each time you extend kindness, your vagus nerve activates and your body releases oxytocin, the "bonding hormone" that helps regulate the nervous system and restore feelings of calm. Each act of kindness becomes a nervous system micro reset, reminding your body that safety and connection can coexist.

Kindness can interrupt inherited messages that say it's not safe to trust others or that vulnerability is weakness. It gently challenges the protective walls built through past experiences.

The Practice

1. Pick something small: It might be as simple as holding the door for someone, offering a sincere compliment, sending a thoughtful text, or leaving a note of gratitude. Choose something that feels both genuine and manageable. The goal is not to perform or overextend, but to engage in a way that feels natural. It shouldn't feel like something that you have to get over with or something that is so high-ticket that it feels stressful.

2. Stay present in the moment and take notice of how your body feels. Did you sense resistance, tightness, or have thoughts like *this is silly* or *they won't even notice*? Observe these sensations with curiosity rather than judgment.

3. Notice what follows, perhaps warmth, ease, or a subtle softening in your chest or face. What emotions or sensations did you feel after your random act of kindness? Did the connection feel safe, unsafe, or neutral? Did the act of kindness challenge any beliefs?

Each act of kindness, no matter how small, is a way of telling your nervous system: *It is safe to connect, to care, and to be seen.* Keep in mind that if this practice begins to feel like self-abandonment, then scale it down. The goal is to feel safe connection, not get into a habit of over-giving.

Journal Prompts

Notice

- What inherited habits, patterns, or beliefs do you notice showing up in your life today? Which of these do you wish to continue carrying forward, and which are you ready to release?

- When do you notice yourself stepping into old family roles, for instance the caretaker, the achiever, or the peacekeeper? What feels familiar about those moments?

Reflect

- Can you identify any trauma loops or survival strategies that your parents or caregivers used to cope with their own life? What purpose did those patterns serve, and have you carried them on in your own life?

- What did you learn you had to *do* to be loved or approved of? What did you learn you had to *hide*?

- When you reflect on the core beliefs you inherited, which shaped your life most strongly? Do any feel outdated or misaligned?

Integrate

- Is there a new belief or pattern you are ready to adopt that feels more authentic to your current self?

- What is one belief, if any, that you want to keep because it truly serves you, and one you're ready to retire with gratitude?

- If you imagine that your ancestors could speak to you from their own experiences, what healing do you think they would wish for you?

Rewiring Your Outlook

I am allowed to change.

Going Forward

As you move forward, notice when your daily choices are being shaped by old patterns. This awareness can loosen their hold. Observe your inherited behaviors and beliefs with compassion, thank them for once keeping you safe, and release them. You can begin to consistently choose authenticity over adaptation, writing new chapters in your story.

As you release these inherited layers and choose from a more authentic place, you may notice something surprising: Even when you want good things, such as rest, joy, ease, and abundance, your body may not feel fully safe receiving them.

In the next chapter, we explore why your nervous system might still brace, contract, or self-protect when life expands. You'll learn how unresolved survival patterns can confuse success with danger, and how rebuilding safety in the body opens the door to receiving more.

—

CHAPTER 4

THE DISCONNECT BETWEEN SAFETY & SUCCESS

Many of us crave growth and expansion but subconsciously associate success with danger. We may consciously want abundance, yet our bodies, still wired for protection, perceive it as a threat. This is because trauma and conditioning can shape our relationship with safety, success, and the ability to receive.

Why Success Can Feel Unsafe

We live in a world that prizes productivity, glorifies burnout, and shames rest unless it has been earned. It is a culture of "more," a world obsessed with acquisition of the biggest, the best, and the newest. Social media amplifies this "look what I have" mentality, where worth is often measured by what can be shown and compared. Often, these external pursuits are attempts to fill internal voids, or soothe our longing for approval, safety, and belonging. The truth is that the nervous system will never find safety through external validation. Until we feel safe within, no amount of achievement or acquisition will fill that space.

From an early age, most of us learned that hustle and achievement is rewarded while rest is equated with weakness. As a result, many of us grow up believing that success equals safety, and that once we finally "arrive," we'll be able to rest, breathe, and feel content and at peace. But the body doesn't wait for a finish line; it only knows how it feels right now. When we withhold permission to rest or feel content until we reach an external milestone, we keep our nervous system locked in survival mode.

Success then becomes a moving target, something that is always slightly out of reach. We chase validation through degrees, promotions, money, possessions, or praise. The more we push from a state of dysregulation, the more dysregulated we become. Over time, exhaustion, stress, and over-functioning feel familiar and therefore "safe."

This is why rest and relaxation can feel so uncomfortable at first. It's not that you are incapable of slowing down, it's that your body doesn't yet recognize rest as safety. Ironically, the safety you seek through achievement becomes unreachable, because on a subconscious level, your nervous system has learned to associate rest, success, and abundance with danger. Stress and overdoing have become familiar and therefore, falsely "safe."

We cannot chase success to earn safety. Safety must be allowed to exist first, here and now. When the nervous system is dysregulated, visibility and success can feel threatening. Being seen, taking up space, or allowing yourself to shine may trigger old fears of criticism, rejection, or loss. So, we stay small, not because we lack ambition, but because the body has learned that expansion equals exposure. You cannot think your way into safety. You must feel your way there.

Why Trauma Blocks Abundance

Trauma shapes how we relate to ourselves, others, and the world. While the mind may crave abundance, the body will only receive what it feels safe to hold. This is the missing piece in many abundance and manifestation teachings: The nervous system must feel safe to receive before expansion can occur.

Trauma-based patterns that we developed can create invisible barriers. These barriers are deep, unconscious beliefs that trace back to early experiences. Love or attention may have been conditional. You might have learned that being quiet, helpful, or invisible kept you safe. Now, as an adult, the act of receiving money, praise, or support can feel unfamiliar or unsafe.

For example, if you grew up in a home where money was a source of tension or scarcity, your nervous system might associate it with danger. You may then unconsciously overspend, lose money easily, hoard, or feel guilty for wanting more.

Common trauma-based money beliefs include:

- *Everything I earn must come through hard work.*
- *If I'm successful, I'll be judged or resented.*
- *Rich people are bad, so money must be bad.*

This discomfort with receiving extends beyond finances. Compliments, generosity, or offers of help can feel triggering when your worth has been tied to performance. Receiving without "earning" can trigger a shame response.

The nervous system does not judge; it categorizes experiences as familiar or unfamiliar. If deprivation, stress, or over-functioning are your baseline, then abundance and ease will feel foreign and therefore unsafe. When opportunities for expansion appear, many people unconsciously self-sabotage or procrastinate. It is the body's way of protecting you from perceived danger.

This is why healing the nervous system is essential for building capacity to expand and receive. How can we receive the abundance that we desire if deep down our bodies do not feel safe to receive it? When safety is restored, abundance flows naturally, not as a performance, but as a state of being.

Patterns That Keep Us Safe (and Small)

Trauma-based patterns often disguise themselves as personality traits. You might notice yourself:

- Being hyper-independent and refusing help, even when you need it
- Over-giving while feeling uncomfortable receiving
- Avoiding visibility or attention
- Feeling shame when you need or want something
- Experiencing overwhelm when things start going well

These are not flaws, they are protective strategies. The nervous system has learned that abundance, ease, and joy mean danger. To shift these patterns, you must first repattern safety in the body so that receiving no longer feels threatening. Once we feel rooted in safety, we can expand in abundance. This is where nervous system wealth begins, in regulation and embodied safety.

Nervous System Reset: Breathwork for the Nervous System

Why does conscious breathing matter? Every breath you take sends a signal to your nervous system, and unlike most automatic body functions, this one can be consciously controlled. This means that you have the ability to shift your entire state of being in just a few minutes.

It's fascinating how subtle changes in timing can create such different effects in the body. The length of each inhale, exhale, and pause sends distinct messages to the nervous system, guiding it toward focus or relaxation. Your breathing patterns are constantly monitored by the body to assess safety. Every variation in your inhale, exhale, and pause are signals to your body. When you consciously lengthen or soften your breath, you are teaching your system that it is safe to rest and receive.

Benefits of Intentional Breathing

- Activates your parasympathetic nervous system
- Lowers your heart rate
- Supports emotional regulation and reduces reactive looping
- Improves focus, sleep, and digestion
- Reduces overwhelm and feelings of uneasiness
- Connects you to the present moment

The Practice

There are many breathing techniques to explore that can support nervous system regulation. Below are a few that can help you regulate your nervous system and reconnect with calm presence. What matters most is not doing them perfectly but taking the time to be intentional about your breath and noticing how your body responds.

Box Breathing

Pattern: Inhale for four counts → hold for four counts → exhale for four counts → hold for four counts, then repeat

Purpose: grounding and emotional regulation

Benefits: creates stability during stress; improves focus; balances activation and relaxation

Best for: moments of overwhelm or grounding before big tasks

4–7–8 Breath

Pattern: Inhale for four counts → hold for seven counts → exhale for eight counts. Initially repeat the cycle up to four times, working up to eight cycles.

Purpose: deep relaxation and preparation for sleep

Benefits: lowers heart rate; activates the vagus nerve; supports sleep readiness; reduces mental tension

Best for: evening unwind, post-stress recovery, or easing anxiety

Long Exhale Breathing

Pattern: Inhale naturally, then extend your exhale to a count of six to eight.

Purpose: quick calming of the nervous system

Benefits: stimulates the parasympathetic response and helps lower cortisol

Best for: grounding after triggers or creating a quick reset between tasks

Breath of Gratitude

Pattern: On each inhale, think the word *thank*; on each exhale, think *you*.

Purpose: cultivating heart coherence and emotional alignment

Benefits: increases heart rate variability; shifts your thoughts toward appreciation; calms the nervous system

Best for: getting centered in the morning; gratitude practices; emotional reset moments

> *Heart Coherence & Heart Rate Variability (HRV)*
> Heart coherence is a state where the heart, brain, and other systems are in harmony, resulting in a greater synchronization between the sympathetic and parasympathetic nervous system, and a shift toward more of a rest and digest state.
>
> HRV is the variation of time between consecutive heartbeats and is one indicator of the body's flexibility under stress. In general, as regulation improves, HRV often improves as well.

Alternate Nostril Breathing

Pattern: Close your right nostril with a finger and then inhale through your left nostril. Close your left nostril, release the right, and exhale through the right. Inhale through the right, close it, and exhale through the left. Repeat for five to ten cycles.

Purpose: balancing and harmonizing the nervous system

Benefits: balances brain hemispheres; clears mental fog; soothes anxiety

Best for: before meditation; before making decisions; anytime you feel off-balance

The Science Behind the Sigh

Taking a deep sigh is your body's natural way of letting go. It is a built-in reset button for your nervous system. A sigh is simply an extended exhale that resets your breathing rhythm, activates vagal calm, and releases physical tension. When you sigh consciously, you give your body permission to pause, soften, and begin again.

After you have tried these different breathing techniques, reflect on your experience. Which pattern felt most accessible to your body, and which felt activating or uncomfortable? What changed in your body after a few moments of intentional breathing?

Journal Prompts

Notice

- Are you able to access moments of safety in your body now? What does that feel like, physically, emotionally, and energetically? Where are you, what are you doing (or not doing), and who are you with when you feel it?

- When you think about receiving more or life getting easier, what sensations arise in your body? Does it feel exciting, tense, undeserved, expanding, or something else? What do you fear will happen next after receiving more?

- What does your nervous system associate with danger: visibility, rest, success, conflict, disappointing someone, outgrowing your role?

Reflect

- What did safety mean to you as a child? Was it something you could rely on, or something that had to be earned through behavior, achievement, or perfection?

- Can you recall specific childhood experiences, people, or conversations that shaped what you believe about safety, love, success, or abundance? Were there clear lessons, spoken or unspoken, about what it meant to "have enough"?

- Can you think of situations where you feel unsafe even though there is no real danger, such as public speaking, being called on unexpectedly, or sharing creative work? Can you trace those feelings back to an early experience when your nervous system learned that visibility was unsafe? (For example: forgetting your words in front of a class and being laughed at.)

Integrate

- What would it look like to pause and acknowledge where you already are instead of moving the target forward?

- What is one form of expansion that you could allow gently instead of avoiding?

Rewiring Your Outlook

Safety is the soil where success can root.

Going Forward

As you move forward, notice how your body responds as you reach toward expansion. It will feel unfamiliar at first, but that does not mean that you are doing something wrong. When discomfort arises, it is often just your nervous system adjusting to a new level of safety. Each time you show your body micro-moments of safety, you teach it that success and ease can coexist. You can rewire your relationship with both safety and abundance, allowing yourself to receive from a grounded, peaceful place instead of survival.

As you continue this work, the next step is learning how to feel somatically safe in your body. Expansion cannot flourish in a body that feels tense, guarded, or braced for impact.

In the next chapter, we explore how physical safety becomes the foundation for emotional openness, intuition, creativity, and authentic expression. When your body begins to root into safety, your capacity for joy, abundance, and aligned action naturally begins to grow.

—

CHAPTER 5

SAFETY AS THE SOIL OF CREATIVE GROWTH

Safety is the foundation for expansion. You cannot create abundance from contraction. You cannot rise and expand until you are rooted in safety.

Your ventral vagal state, the part of your nervous system associated with creativity, connection, and presence, becomes far more accessible when your body feels safe. You can build success from a stressed, sympathetic state, but it will likely feel hard and unsustainable.

To truly thrive, your body must learn that ease is not a threat and that visibility is not dangerous. This requires gentle rewiring: learning to pause, breathe, receive, and trust that your worth is not measured by your output. When your body trusts that it is safe to rest, to receive, and to be seen, success becomes a natural expression of that safety.

Safety as Creative Soil

Our creative energy cannot flourish without a supported and regulated nervous system. When we live in survival mode, the body directs its resources toward protection, not creation. Even if we have creative visions or ambitious goals, we can feel paralyzed and unable to act. This often leads to frustration, disappointment, and self-criticism.

We may wonder why we can't bring our ideas to life while others seem to do it effortlessly. The truth is, we are not flawed or lazy, we are simply protecting ourselves. Healing begins when we replace judgment with compassion and give ourselves permission to go slowly. As we gently rewire our nervous system, what once felt dangerous begins to feel safe. In this new soil of safety, creative energy can bloom.

When I am dysregulated, feeling anxious, overstimulated, or tense, I often feel a block in my creative flow. In the past, my mind would flood with self-criticism. Now I know those thoughts are simply echoes of a stressed nervous system. Instead of spiraling, I pause, breathe, and ground, reminding myself that *I am safe in this moment.* I anchor back into my body before I create.

Relearning Safety

So how do we rewire the nervous system to feel safe? Initially, we start with small moments. We allow ourselves to enjoy a cup of tea without multitasking. We speak up when we might have stayed silent. We are conscious of the moment and intentional. We take a deep breath and remind ourselves: *right now, I am safe. Nothing bad is happening.*

From there, we can branch out to more small moments of trust, while staying present and aware. We place a hand on the heart or belly and notice the breath. We feel the ground beneath our feet, anchoring into that space. These simple acts remind the body that the present moment is safe, even if the past once was not.

Another step in this healing process is allowing space for what we once denied ourselves. We can give ourselves permission to cry, to rest, to set boundaries, and to receive support. Each of these moments offers the body a chance to heal old wounds. The goal is not perfection, it is awareness, noticing when we've slipped into dysregulation and gently guiding ourselves back to regulation with grace and compassion.

Observing the Emotion

Observing emotions is not detachment; rather, it is presence without judgment. It means allowing yourself to feel fully while remembering that every emotion is temporary. Emotions are messengers, revealing where something within you needs care or attention.

You do not have to embody the feeling. When you notice a sense of activation or discomfort, pause and observe instead of reacting. You are not the emotion; you are just experiencing it in that moment.

Do not bury the feeling or let it explode. Instead, name the emotion without becoming it: *I am feeling anxious*, not *I am anxious*. That subtle shift reminds your body that emotions are an experience, not a part of your identity. You are not anger; you are someone who feels angry, and that feeling will pass. Recognize. Observe. Explore. Then let it move through you.

This simple shift helps you remember that emotions are just energy in motion. They pass through, but they do not define who you are. Once you name what you're feeling, approach it with curiosity rather than judgment: *What is this emotion trying to tell me?* Show your body that it is safe to experience it without judgment, so that you can let the emotion pass through you without fighting against it.

This exploration allows you to pinpoint what is bothering you from a rational thought process rather than a triggered emotional reaction. By observing rather than identifying with the emotion, you interrupt the shame loop and create space for new, regulated responses. This is how awareness becomes healing.

Anchoring Safety

As moments of safety, joy, and peace arise, pause and honor them. Notice how they feel in your body. Breathe them in. This awareness anchors safety into your nervous system. With time and repetition, you can build a new baseline for your life, one where you are not just surviving, but thriving.

Nervous System Reset: Open Palms Meditation

The purpose of this practice is to symbolically open your body's ability to receive through a physical change of posture. You will move your body from a more closed and defensive stance to one that is open and receptive. This is another way to gently show the nervous system that we can associate receiving with safety and nourishment.

When the nervous system has spent years bracing, we often subconsciously position our bodies in crossed arms, tight shoulders, shallow breath, or clenched fists. This is signaling our nervous system that we are not open to receiving because it feels threatening rather than nourishing.

By intentionally softening your body positions and opening the palms, you invite your nervous system into a state of receptivity. You show your body that openness does not mean danger, restoring the body's ability to receive and opening the possibilities of abundance and connection.

The Practice

1. Find a comfortable seated position. Relax your jaw and let your shoulders soften.

2. Place your hands face down on your knees. Notice any subtle tension in your arms, hands, or breath.

3. Take several slow, grounding breaths. Inhale to lengthen your spine. Exhale to release tension through your shoulders.

4. On your next inhale, gently soften your fingers. Turn your palms upward, resting the back of your hands on your knees. Allow the palms to open without forcing them.

5. With each inhale, imagine soft energy flowing into your chest and down your arms into your palms. With each exhale, imagine releasing anything that blocks you from receiving.

6. Repeat softly, either aloud or internally: *It is safe for me to receive. I am open to love, possibility, and abundance.*

7. Pause and notice. How does your body respond to this posture change? Does anything soften? Does anything resist? Does saying *I am open to receiving* bring ease or tightness?

Why This Works

Closed postures send subtle cues for protection and defensiveness. Your body is preparing itself for threat, not expansion. Open postures communicate safety and capacity, restoring the body's ability to receive. This small physical shift can create a profound emotional and energetic shift. Take notice when your body is tightening, and take a few seconds to recenter, ground, and soften.

Journal Prompts

Notice

- When you feel safe, what signals does your body give you? When you feel unsafe, what changes?

- If your body could speak, what would it say it needs to feel supported, grounded, or safe right now?

- What emotion has been showing up most often for you lately? What message might it be trying to deliver?

Reflect

- What does safety mean to you beyond the physical sense: emotionally, spiritually, energetically?

- When an emotion arises, what is your first instinct: to fix it, avoid it, or feel it? What might that pattern be trying to protect you from? What emotions feel easiest for you to express, and which ones do you tend to suppress or avoid?

- Can you recall a recent moment when you were flooded with emotion? What would have happened if you had paused to observe it instead of reacting?

Integrate

- Are there places, people, or activities that help your nervous system settle? How can you invite more of those into your routine?

- If you were to intentionally cultivate more safety in your daily life, what would that look like? What small steps could you begin with?

Rewiring Your Outlook

I am safe to create, express, and expand.

Going Forward

As you move forward, remember that safety is not something you have to earn. It is something you can gently reclaim, moment by moment. The body does not heal through force; it softens through permission. Every time you pause, breathe, and choose awareness over self-criticism, you are showing your nervous system that peace is possible.

Keep returning to small, simple acts of safety. These moments might seem insignificant, but they are the roots from which expansion grows. As your body learns that safety and creativity can coexist, you may find that inspiration flows more freely and self-trust deepens. You no longer create from a place of fear or needing to prove yourself. Safety is not the absence of challenge; it's the inner knowing that you can meet life with steadiness and grace.

As your body begins to experience safety again, you may also notice deeper emotions rising to the surface, old patterns, buried memories, or parts of yourself you learned to hide. This is not regression; it is the natural next layer of healing. When safety takes root, the mind finally feels resourced enough to reveal what has been eclipsed by survival.

In the next chapter, I invite you to meet these hidden parts with compassion rather than fear. Here, you will explore how to gently illuminate the unconscious patterns that shape your reactions and how to integrate the emotions you once pushed away. This is where self-awareness deepens and self-connection strengthens.

———

CHAPTER 6

SHADOW WORK
& EMOTIONAL INTEGRATION

Don't cry. Babies cry. Are you a baby?
Stop complaining. You should feel lucky.
Knock it off. You have no right to be upset.
You deserved it.

Most of us have heard some version of these words growing up, and each one taught us, either subtly or directly, to suppress our emotions. These emotions became hidden, creating our shadow side. The shadow side of us is not something bad. It is simply what has been hidden. Our shadow can hold ancestral shame, parts of ourselves we learned to disown, as well as suppressed emotions like anger, fear, jealousy, rage, sadness, and even desire or joy.

We learned early in our lives which emotions were acceptable to express, and which were not. Perhaps when you showed joy, anger, or vulnerability, it led to rejection or punishment, and so you learned to push those emotions deep into the shadows. Our bodies store these unexpressed energies and, over time, they can become contributing roots of nervous system dysregulation.

Shadow work is the process of gently bringing these hidden parts into awareness, meeting them with compassion rather than judgment. Integration happens not by forgetting or erasing the past but by allowing it to flow through us, witnessed with presence and love. When we do this, the nervous system begins to find harmony and coherence. Shadow work invites us to heal past traumas and move toward deeper self-acceptance and self-love.

Signs You May Benefit from Shadow Work

- You react with strong emotions when triggered. These reactions, such as anger, jealousy, fear, or shame, often point to something unresolved within you.

- You repeat similar toxic patterns in relationships. You find yourself in the same dynamics, even with different people.

- You consistently self-sabotage. You hold yourself back from real growth through distraction, procrastination, or unproductive habits.

- Your self-talk is harsh. It is filled with judgment or shame.

- You overreact to the behaviors of others. You especially react to traits you secretly reject in yourself (for example, calling someone "too selfish" or "too emotional").

- You feel empty or disconnected. You feel like you're moving through life on autopilot without joy or purpose.

- You fear being truly seen. You hide your authentic self to avoid rejection or embarrassment.

- You rely on external coping mechanisms. You use things like food, spending, work, substances, or endless scrolling to avoid emotional discomfort.

- You resist stillness or are bothered by quiet. You keep yourself busy in order to avoid the thoughts or feelings that might surface. You avoid any self-reflection.

- You idolize or demonize others. You do not realize that you are projecting parts of yourself, perhaps parts that you don't want to see in yourself, onto them.

Shadow work helps you reclaim the disowned parts of yourself. It is not about fixing what is broken but about remembering what was forgotten. By bringing compassion to your shadows, you create integration, and that integration allows your nervous system to relax, your creativity to return, and your wholeness to emerge.

Perhaps you have already begun the practice. Shadow work is often misunderstood as something dramatic, intense, or intimidating, but most shadow work is a more subtle, lived experience. You have likely already been doing it in ways you haven't recognized, showing up in the ways you move through your daily life. Here are signs that your inner work is already unfolding.

Signs You've Already Been Doing Shadow Work

1. You can laugh at yourself. Your attachment to being "perfect" or always right has softened. You can see your patterns with tenderness, sometimes even humor, without collapsing into shame.

2. You are less easily triggered. People or situations that once sent you spiraling no longer hold the same power. You pause before reacting and often respond to the discomfort of being triggered with curiosity rather than defensiveness.

3. You take responsibility without overidentifying. You can acknowledge mistakes, missteps, or reactive moments without spiraling into guilt or shame. You hold yourself accountable and give yourself room to grow.

4. You can hold space for the emotions of others. You no longer feel responsible for fixing or rescuing, and you no longer take things personally when someone else expresses difficult feelings. You stay grounded, even when the emotional atmosphere is intense.

5. You have befriended parts of yourself you once rejected. You no longer hide from your anger, jealousy, neediness, or sensitivity. Instead of exiling these parts, you understand their roots and listen to what they are trying to tell you.

6. You no longer demonize or idolize others. You see people as nuanced, complex, and layered, not just all good or all bad. This includes parents, partners, friends, teachers, exes, and even past versions of yourself.

7. You feel safe being seen in your authenticity. You are no longer overexplaining, shapeshifting, or performing for approval. Visibility feels less like danger and more like freedom.

8. You set boundaries without guilt. You have learned that saying no, resting, or protecting your peace is not selfish. Boundaries now feel like self-respect rather than conflict, and so you no longer betray yourself to avoid disappointing others.

9. You notice patterns and work with them instead of against them. When an old behavior resurfaces, you don't spiral into shame. You treat it as a doorway to deeper understanding and compassion.

10. You have more compassion for the shadow in others. You recognize that everyone has a shadow, and that judgment is often a reflection of pain. You approach others with softer eyes and stronger discernment.

If you recognize any of these signs in yourself, you are already engaging in meaningful shadow work. While these shifts are powerful, they're only the beginning. We will soon explore the skills that deepen this integration: recognizing triggers and emotional patterns with clarity; establishing and holding boundaries as an act of self-respect; taking responsibility without self-blame; and moving from reactivity into conscious choice. These are the practices that transform shadow work from emotional awareness into embodied self-worth, forming a solid foundation for what follows in this book.

Nervous System Reset: Mirror Gazing for Self-Compassion

As we explored in this chapter, we can often be our own harshest critic. Our inner dialogue can become unkind, echoing shame, guilt, or disappointment that we have carried for years. Sometimes, just one glance at our reflection can trigger cycles of negative self-talk.

This practice aims to gently rewire the way you speak to yourself, to slowly regain safety in perceiving ourselves in a positive way. You are teaching your nervous system that you can feel seen and loved.

The Practice

1. Find a quiet space where you can be alone for a few minutes. Prepare the atmosphere in a way that feels soothing: Soften the lights. Light a candle, or just keep it simple.

2. Take a few slow, grounding breaths, then slowly meet your own gaze in the mirror. Resist the familiar urge to judge. Just see yourself as you are. When you initially look into your own eyes, what do you notice: judgment, curiosity, disappointment, discomfort? What might those first impressions be teaching you about your current capacity for self-love?

3. What emotions surface when you hold your own gaze without looking away? Where do you feel them in your body? If looking deeply into your eyes feels uncomfortable, honor that. If you need to stop there for now, that's perfectly okay. You can return when you feel ready.

4. Imagine your reflection representing all versions of you: child, adolescent, and then adult. What does each one need to hear right now? In a calm, kind voice, say whatever you most need to hear in this moment. It might be as simple as: *I can see that you are tired. You deserve to rest*, or *I am so proud of you.*

5. Allow yourself to receive your own words with compassion. You can place your hands on your heart if that feels like the right thing to do.

6. When you are ready to close your practice, offer yourself a soft smile. Say to your reflection: *Thank you. I love you.*

After completing your mirror gazing practice, take a few slow breaths and notice what arises within you. How does your body feel? Do you sense any softening, resistance, or emotion surfacing? Simply observe these sensations with curiosity rather than judgment. This is your nervous system learning that presence with yourself can be safe.

This simple yet powerful ritual helps retrain your body and mind to associate self-recognition with safety and warmth. Over time, it transforms the mirror from a source of judgment into a place of acceptance and love.

Journal Prompts

Notice

- Which emotions are the most difficult for you to feel fully right now and why? Which emotion tends to linger the longest before you can release it? Why do you think that this one sticks with you longer?

- How do you typically respond to your own mistakes or emotional intensity? Can you recall a time when you judged yourself for an emotional reaction?

- Can you remember specific times when you began to hide pieces of yourself away? Where in your body do you feel those memories or emotions now?

Reflect

- What emotions were discouraged or unsafe to express when you were growing up?

- Which parts of yourself have you learned to hide or down-play in order to feel accepted or safe?

- Think of a time when you overreacted or completely shut down. What might be asking for attention beneath the surface? Can you connect that reaction to a younger version of yourself? What might that younger self have needed in that moment?

Integrate

- How might compassion change the way you remember or respond to your emotional reactions?

- What does it feel like to imagine welcoming all parts of yourself instead of managing or correcting them?

Rewiring Your Outlook

I honor every part of me.

Going Forward

As you continue this work, remember that healing is not about erasing your shadows but embracing them. Each emotion, reaction, or memory that surfaces is an invitation to reclaim another part of yourself. The more you meet your hidden parts with compassion, the less power they hold over you. Continue to offer yourself patience and kindness as you explore what was once hidden. This is the heart of integration: learning to feel safe in the full truth of who you are.

As you meet your shadows with more gentleness, you may notice the subtle ways they show up in your daily life: in your reactions, your relationships, and the moments when your body tenses before your mind understands why. These are your patterns, your triggers, and the emotional loops that you have carried for years.

In the next chapter, we turn toward these signals with curiosity rather than judgment. This will help you understand why certain situations still activate old wounds, how your body communicates through emotion, and how awareness becomes the first step toward breaking automatic cycles. By learning to name what arises, you begin to transform reactivity into choice, and choice into deeper emotional freedom.

CHAPTER 7

RECOGNIZING TRIGGERS, PATTERNS & EMOTIONS

We learned in an earlier chapter that, throughout our lives, we unconsciously take on certain roles like the people-pleaser, the martyr, or the responsible one. These roles were born from the environments we grew up in and the messages we absorbed about what made us lovable or safe. They were never mistakes; they were adaptive. They were the ways our nervous system learned to keep us secure in the world, but these same roles can keep us trapped in pattern cycles.

Our patterns are not proof of failure; they are evidence of survival. Each one began as an intelligent adaptation to feeling unsafe, unseen, or unworthy. A child who stayed quiet to avoid punishment may grow into an adult who struggles to speak up. A child who learned that love had to be earned may become an adult who overperforms, or maybe they never feel like they are enough.

These patterns were once forms of protection. They helped us navigate uncertain environments, find a sense of belonging, and minimize danger. But what once kept us safe is also keeping us small. When we recognize our patterns with compassion rather than shame, we can see them for what they are—survival strategies that have simply outlived their purpose.

Awareness is the first step toward transformation. By noticing how our patterns show up in our life, we create the opportunity to pause, reflect, and choose differently. This is how we move from unconscious repetition to conscious design.

What It Means to Get Triggered

Being triggered doesn't mean that you are broken or that you are overly sensitive; it means that your nervous system is remembering. A trigger is your body's way of signaling that something in the present moment feels similar to a past experience where safety was lost. Your mind may see a harmless situation, but your body responds as though danger is near.

When a trigger arises, your heart may race, your breath shortens, or your muscles tense before you even have time to think. The body is not overreacting; it is protecting. Every trigger is an echo of a moment when you didn't feel safe, a doorway into deeper understanding.

When you recognize what a triggered reaction feels like in yourself, you also notice it in others. This awareness naturally brings empathy. You see that most people are walking through the world in various states of activation, still carrying the echoes of their own unhealed pain. Compassion for yourself and others is what breaks the cycle.

From Reaction to Choice

When you get to a place where you are recognizing your own triggers, patterns, and emotions, you can pause and decide whether you are going to again react from that same place or perhaps make a different choice this time. There is a real feeling of freedom when we realize that we can decide from a new level of heightened awareness how we want to react and move forward. We are taking an active role in our life rather than allowing life to happen to us. Holding space for yourself in this way is an act of sovereignty. It is how you stop reacting to life and start responding to it with awareness.

Why It Feels So Personal & Why It Isn't

Every person experiences life through a unique lens shaped by belief, experience, and trauma. We often assume others see the world as we do, but we are all navigating through different realities filtered by our own nervous system responses. Many are not even aware that they are carrying these patterns and triggers. They project an air of arrogance or overconfidence to protect their own ego. They can lash out at others, bully, or belittle for their own self-preservation.

When we lack self-worth, we tend to take these actions of others personally. We absorb their projections as truth, yet much of what others say or do has nothing to do with us at all. It reflects their own pain. Bullying, judgment, and criticism are often expressions of someone else's unresolved fear and traumas.

We really can have no idea what kind of life experience another person has had. Recognizing this truth doesn't excuse harm, but it does protect your sense of self-worth. Then we can make a conscious effort to try and understand where another person might be coming from.

At times, our own wounds distort our perceptions. We misinterpret neutral interactions as rejection or threat because our body is reading them through an old filter. When this happens, gently ask yourself, *Is this still true for me?* This simple question invites the possibility of a new lens, one shaped by compassion, awareness, and new feelings of safety.

When emotions surge, it may feel impossible to think rationally. This is not a failure on our part; it is literally our biology at work. Your body senses a threat and so automatically shifts into survival mode:

- The amygdala detects a potential threat and sounds the alarm.

- Adrenaline and cortisol flood your system.

- Blood flow diverts away from the prefrontal cortex, the part of your brain responsible for logic and communication.

- You move into fight, flight, or freeze.

Your body is prioritizing safety, not reasoning. That's why grounding practices, like deep breathing, are essential when you feel triggered. They signal to the body that the threat has passed and allow you to return to calm.

The Power of the Pause

A trigger is not a setback; it is a moment of awareness where change becomes possible. The moment you notice a trigger, you are no longer inside the pattern, you are observing it.

Once we are in the habit of noticing when we become triggered, then getting triggered can be viewed as a positive thing in a way. When you stay curious rather than judgmental, every trigger becomes an opportunity to meet yourself more deeply, explore yourself, give attention where it is needed, and continue to heal.

The moment you notice you've been triggered, you can pause and ask yourself: *What about this situation or that person's words bothered me so much and why?* You may have to ask "why" several times, peeling back layers until you reach the root. If you don't find an answer right away, that's okay. Sometimes you may not know why something bothers you, but at least you have the chance to reflect. You can continue to peel back the layers, learning more and more about yourself.

With time, you will recognize triggers sooner, recover faster, and respond with greater awareness. Each pause and each deep breath retrain your nervous system to associate awareness with safety so awareness itself becomes a healing practice.

Nervous System Reset: Grounding & Earthing

You may be familiar with grounding as the practice of standing barefoot on the earth. While this is one form of grounding, in this book we'll distinguish between grounding and earthing. Grounding refers to the more general practice of bringing awareness back to the present moment. You are getting out of your head, reconnecting with your body, and rooting into presence. Earthing is the physical practice of connecting your bare skin to the surface of the Earth.

The Benefits of Grounding

Grounding helps orient the body to the present moment, calm the body's stress response and restore balance to the nervous system. Some of the key benefits of grounding include:

- Calms the body's stress response and reduces feelings of overwhelm
- Regulates heart rate and breathing
- Relaxes muscular tension
- Improves focus and decision-making
- Lowers cortisol levels
- Heightens awareness of internal sensations
- Enhances self-regulation, making it easier to respond instead of react
- Signals safety and stability to the brain

When you are grounded, you feel calm, centered, and connected to your surroundings. You are aware of your boundaries, attuned to your body, and feel safe to rest.

Grounding can take many forms: mindful breathing, sensory awareness, visualization, or physical contact with nature. You can weave these practices into your daily routine.

Earthing: Connecting with the Earth's Energy

Earthing involves making direct skin contact with the Earth's surface through your bare feet, hands, or other parts of your body, touching soil, grass, sand, or water. The simple act of physical contact with the ground can be deeply regulating for the nervous system, especially when the body has been living in a state of chronic alert. The sensory feedback of contact with the earth can signal stability, containment, and safety, allowing the body to settle more easily.

The Practice

When you take the time to ground or connect physically with the Earth, you send a clear message to your body: *I am safe in this moment*. Each practice gently resets the nervous system and invites you back into balance, one breath and one barefoot step at a time.

- Stand barefoot on grass, soil, sand, or stone for ten to twenty minutes each day.

- Submerge your feet in natural water, such as a lake or ocean, or take a mindful swim if you can.

- Sit or lie directly on the ground. Combine this with another calming practice, such as journaling or meditation.

- Garden with your bare hands in the soil. Skip the gloves to experience the full grounding effect.

- If outdoor access is limited, grounding mats or sheets can be used indoors to simulate the Earth's energy field.

Journal Prompts

Notice

- Can you recall specific situations where you felt triggered, or moments when your emotional response felt strong or disproportionate? What sensations did you notice in your body?

- Do you notice recurring protection patterns, such as people-pleasing, withdrawing, overworking, or deflecting with humor? Which patterns appear most often, and in what kinds of situations?

- When you are triggered, what feels most at risk: connection, safety, belonging, or worth? What does your nervous system seem to believe will happen if you don't react the way you usually do?

Reflect

- Is there a particular emotion that feels difficult for you to express, such as anger, sadness, or fear? If so, what makes it uncomfortable or unsafe? Were you ever taught to suppress this feeling?

- Are there people, situations, or environments that consistently trigger you? What is the first emotion that arises? If you dig a little deeper, what might that reaction really be about? (For example, "When I feel dismissed at work, it touches an old feeling of being unseen as a child.")

- After a trigger passes, what do you tend to replay or fixate on? What might you be trying to resolve, protect, or understand?

Integrate

- What conditions help your body return to regulation the fastest and which ones are actually prolonging activation even if they look helpful, for example, venting, overprocessing, or seeking reassurance?

- If you imagine your next trigger as a doorway rather than an interruption, what might it be inviting you to notice, feel, or choose differently?

Rewiring Your Outlook

I can witness my emotions without being consumed by them.

Going Forward

Awareness of your triggers and patterns is not meant to create judgment; it is an invitation to meet yourself with compassion. As you continue this work, remember that regulation is built through repetition. The small, consistent moments when you choose to pause instead of react, to ground instead of spiral, are what rewire your nervous system over time. Each time you reconnect with your body, you are creating new roots of safety, deep enough to hold your expansion, creativity, and peace.

As your awareness deepens, you may notice the weight you still carry from past wounds, moments where your body learned to brace, protect, or harden. These imprints do not dissolve through logic alone; they require tenderness, presence, and a way of relating to the past that brings the body back into safety.

In the next chapter, we explore forgiveness not as a cognitive decision but as a nervous system process. You will learn how the body stores unresolved hurt, how releasing it creates space for regulation, and how forgiveness, whether directed inward or outward, becomes a pathway to freedom. This chapter invites you to soften, to let your body exhale what it has held for too long, and to experience forgiveness as a way to prepare your body for expansion.

CHAPTER 8

THE SOMATIC LANGUAGE
OF FORGIVENESS

Forgiveness can be one of the most profound healings that our nervous system can experience. It is not a polite social gesture or a simple exchange of words. Rather, it is a deep, embodied process that frees our body from the tension of the past. We often think of forgiveness as something we owe others, but in truth, forgiveness is something we offer ourselves so that we can reclaim our peace, our energy, and our sense of safety in the present moment. We can alchemize our past experiences into wisdom that supports the future we desire.

Forgiveness as Nervous System Regulation

Culturally, we've been taught a transactional version of forgiveness. Someone says, "I'm sorry," and we're expected to respond, "It's okay," even when our body knows it's not. We may still be hurting, or maybe we know that the apology was not genuine, which is often the case when apologies are forced. We are told to move on, to be the bigger person, to keep the peace. Yet inside, the body still clenches. The muscles tighten, the breath shortens, and the nervous system stays braced as if the hurt might happen again.

This happens because forgiveness cannot be forced by the mind. It must be felt in the body on a deeper level. True forgiveness is not about excusing behavior or pretending that someone's words or actions did not hurt. It is not about forgetting or reconciling with someone who is unsafe. Forgiveness is about releasing the grip that pain has on your nervous system so that your body no longer flinches at the memory.

When you forgive, you are not saying, "What happened was okay." You are saying, "I refuse to carry this pain any longer." Forgiveness is a somatic act of liberation. You are freeing yourself from the loop that replays the memory, leading to more hurt feelings and resentment. It softens the tension that you have been carrying. When the body begins to relax around an old wound, energy that was once trapped in survival becomes available for creativity, joy, and peace.

You may not feel ready to forgive all at once, and that's okay. Forgiveness is a practice, one small release at a time. Each repetition loosens the body's grip on the past, allowing the nervous system to find safety in the present.

The Practice of Self-Forgiveness

We often forget to include ourselves in forgiveness. We are quick to hold compassion for others, yet we criticize ourselves endlessly. When we make mistakes, we are incredibly hard on ourselves. We remember the relationships we stayed in too long, the boundaries we didn't set, the coping mechanisms we turned to, and the times we didn't speak up, and we carry shame for those moments.

But each of those choices was an act of survival. Your body and your nervous system were doing the best they could with the resources they had at the time. What may look like a mistake through the lens of hindsight was, in truth, an attempt to find safety.

Self-forgiveness invites you to release the judgment around how you adapted in the past. It asks you to meet yourself, the version that endured, that kept going, that did whatever it needed to do, with tenderness instead of blame. Forgiving yourself is not about letting yourself "off the hook," it is about acknowledging your humanity. It is about softening the critical voice within and allowing compassion to rewire your inner dialogue.

Each time you practice self-forgiveness, you are sending safety signals to your nervous system, reminding it that you no longer need to live in defense against yourself. Over time, this softens the edges of self-judgment and opens the heart to deeper self-love.

Nervous System Reset: Forgiveness Ritual

The practice of forgiveness can bring profound peace to the body. Forgiving is not about condoning harmful behavior or pretending that what happened was acceptable. It is an energetic release, a conscious decision to free your body from the tension, anger, and resentment it has been carrying. We are liberating the body from the ongoing stress that is caused by holding onto resentment and anger.

When you forgive, you are not doing it for the other person; you are doing it for your own nervous system. Each act of forgiveness signals to the body that the experience that you are forgiving no longer has any control over you, and so the body no longer needs to remain in a state of defense or stress. Through this release, you invite safety, rest, and softness back into your internal landscape.

This forgiveness ritual will help your body complete an unfinished stress cycle and move toward peace. Take your time. This process is deeply personal and can be approached as gently or as gradually as you need. And remember, you are doing this practice for your benefit; the words are not spoken to the other person.

The Practice

1. Create space for stillness. Choose a time when you can be uninterrupted for a few minutes. If you feel drawn to shorter sessions, you can do this practice in stages. You could also do one person or memory for each practice. Forgiveness is not a one-time act; it unfolds in layers.

2. Prepare your environment. Find a calm, comfortable place to sit. Have a pen and paper ready.

3. Center your breath. Close your eyes and take several slow, grounding breaths. Feel your body soften as you exhale. Notice any tension that arises.

4. When you are ready, write your list. Begin by naming the person, situation, or version of yourself that you are ready to release. Write what happened, how it made you feel, and the emotions connected to it. Then write the words: "I forgive you."

5. Let emotion move through you. You may cry, feel anger, or notice sensations in your body. Allow it. This is your nervous system processing stored energy. You can pause whenever you need to and return when you feel ready.

6. Bring closure. When you have completed your list, read it silently or quietly to yourself. Take a few deep breaths and imagine what this deep forgiveness feels like in your body. Then, tear, bury, or safely burn your list as a symbolic act of release.

7. Integrate and observe. Sit quietly for a moment and notice any sensations in your body. Were some memories easier to release than others?

Offer gratitude to yourself for being willing to let go, even a little. Each time you release a layer of resentment, you make more space for peace.

Often these memories want to be seen for a reason, likely because something has not been processed. See it with gentleness and compassion. Remind yourself that you are safe in this moment. This memory does not have to hurt you anymore. It is in the past. When you consciously bring your nervous system back into a regulated state when these memories come up, you are showing your nervous system that you are safe. Over time, the goal is not to erase the memory, but for the body to no longer react as if the danger is still present. You haven't forgotten it, but it no longer has a hold over you, and you are no longer having a nervous system response.

Journal Prompts

Notice

- When a painful memory surfaces, how does your body respond? Where do you feel it? What happens with your breath, posture, or muscle tension?

- When you think about the act of forgiving, what sensations arise in your body? Does it feel light, tense, resistant, or peaceful?

- What does self-forgiveness feel like in your body? Does it bring relief, grief, warmth, or something else entirely?

Reflect

- Is there a habit or trait that you find yourself reacting strongly to in others? If you look deeper, can you see this as a reflection of something within yourself that needs compassion rather than judgment?

- How have you punished yourself for past decisions, relationships, or failures? What did you need back then that you didn't receive?

Integrate

- What parts of yourself have you been withholding forgiveness from? What would it feel like to extend compassion and forgiveness to those parts now?

- What is one thing you continue to replay in your mind, for instance a regret, mistake, or missed opportunity, that you are ready to release today?

- If your younger self could hear you now, what words of forgiveness or reassurance would you offer?

Rewiring Your Outlook

Forgiveness gives me freedom.

Going Forward

Forgiveness is not a single act. Each time you choose to release even a small piece of resentment, your body learns that it no longer needs to live in protection. Allow yourself to forgive at your own pace, without forcing closure. Remember, this work is not about forgetting what happened; it is about reclaiming the energy that has been tied to the pain. Each breath of compassion, each gentle act of release, signals to your nervous system that it is safe to let go, safe to rest, and safe to live with an open heart again.

As you complete this chapter, you stand at a meaningful turning point. You have rooted into safety, met your shadows, softened old defenses, and practiced releasing what your body no longer needs to hold.

Before stepping into the next section, pause and check in with yourself. There is no rush. If you feel uncertain or not quite ready to move forward, it might simply mean you are still rooting. You'll recognize readiness to rise when there is a subtle steadiness within you and a quiet curiosity about what is possible—when you begin to sense that you have a say in what comes next.

With this foundation in place, you are ready to enter *Building from Safety into Self-Trust*. Here, the work begins to shift. Instead of simply understanding where your patterns came from, you begin to shape what comes next.

In the next chapter, we explore how the narratives you inherited, absorbed, or repeated in moments of pain have shaped your identity, and how to rewrite them from a place of regulation and truth. This chapter invites you to step into authorship of your life: not by erasing the past, but by reclaiming the pen. As you move forward, you are no longer defined by what happened to you; you are defined by the story you choose to live from now on.

RISE

—

*Building from
Safety into Self-Trust*

—

CHAPTER 9

REWRITING YOUR STORY

Feeling powerless, feeling small, feeling like life is something that just happens to us—these are not fixed realities. They are mindsets that can shift. Healing begins when we stop blaming and start becoming aware of the stories that we have been telling ourselves. Some of these stories we can trace back to people, moments, or memories. Other stories may feel harder to locate as they are patterns so deeply woven into our identity that they seem to have no beginning.

I carried an immense amount of guilt and shame around rest and relaxation. I felt like an utter disappointment when I wasn't accomplishing enough, like I was letting myself and my family down. Surrounded by seemingly high-functioning people, I wondered why I couldn't keep up. I still don't know exactly where that belief originated, maybe generational imprints, maybe societal pressure that I internalized. But I finally realized that it was there, and that awareness was the first step toward healing that wound.

I stopped worrying about judgment for taking a break or putting my feet up in the middle of the day. I reframed my thinking: Rest wasn't laziness, it was restoration. I began to see that I could give more to the people I love when my own cup was full. In doing so, I set a better example, one rooted in honoring the body and its needs.

Reframing the Stories We Tell Ourselves

We carry stories about who we are, what we deserve, and what's possible for us. Many of these stories were written for us before we even had a voice. As children, we needed love and safety more than authenticity. We learned to stay quiet instead of honest, to put on a brave face instead of showing fear. These survival strategies later hardened into identities.

Realizing this gives us choice. We can rewrite the chapters of our past, not by changing what happened, but by changing how we understand it. When we pull our stories out from behind the lens of shame or victimhood and view them through compassion, the entire meaning shifts. That is how we begin writing our next chapter from a place of embodied worthiness.

Uncovering Limiting Beliefs

Limiting beliefs are simply stories. They are old scripts about ourselves, others, or how we experience the world. They restrict what we believe to be possible and keep us small. Many are inherited, passed quietly from one generation to the next. They might sound like:

> *I'm just not good at that.*
>
> *People like me never succeed.*
>
> *I don't deserve love.*
>
> *There's no point in trying; I'll just fail.*

Over time, these beliefs become our inner dialogue, and they shift to "I am," becoming a part of our identity.

I am unworthy.

I am a failure.

I am broken.

When we repeat these stories to ourselves often enough, they become ingrained in our bodies and in our nervous system. Once these statements are fully embodied, it becomes difficult to do anything that might prove them wrong. "It's just who I am," we say, and stop reaching. Stop expanding. Stop trying. But these stories can be rewritten. First, we notice them. Then, we reframe them. We begin to tell new stories:

I am worthy.

I deserve love.

I can learn.

I am enough.

Be patient with yourself as you practice this. It takes time to untangle a lifetime of criticism and conditioning. As you realize that limiting beliefs are just stories, not truths, you reclaim your power to write something new.

The Power of Words

The stories we tell ourselves become our reality, but they are not set in stone. For years, I used to say, "I'm terrible with names." And guess what? I was. When I stopped saying it and rewrote the story, I began remembering names easily. It's a simple example, but a profound truth: The language we use shapes our identity and our reality.

I'm not creative.

I'm not smart enough.

I'll never change.

These are not facts; they are narratives. And the more we repeat them, the more our nervous system registers them as truth. They become embodied responses, felt in the body long before they're spoken aloud.

You have the power to change that story, to choose how you want to walk through life, the kind of person you want to be, and the example you want to set. You can rewrite your story, one word, one thought, one compassionate moment at a time.

Rewriting from Embodied Worthiness

So, what new story feels true for you now? What narrative feels aligned with your authentic self? When you imagine life without the constraints of your old stories and limiting beliefs, you can almost feel your nervous system exhale. The blinders fall away. You can see the possibilities stretching out before you. You get to decide what the next chapter looks like. You get to write the story of your healing, your becoming, your worth. There are infinite possibilities waiting to be discovered. The question is: Which path will you take next?

Nervous System Reset: Releasing That Which No Longer Serves You Ritual

This ritual offers a ceremonial way to release the old stories, patterns, and identities that no longer align with who you are becoming. When the body and mind are ready to evolve, these outdated beliefs can feel heavy, like emotional residue weighing you down. This practice provides both symbolic and somatic closure, allowing you to gently tell your nervous system it's safe to let go now.

The Practice

1. Prepare your space. Choose a time and place where you can be alone for a few quiet moments. You might light a candle, play soft music, or keep things simple and still. Create an atmosphere that feels supportive and authentic to you. If the environment feels forced, the body won't fully relax into the ritual. Have a pen and paper ready.

2. Ground yourself. Take several slow, deep breaths. Feel your body's connection to the floor beneath you. Allow your shoulders to soften and focus on your breath. This helps signal safety to the nervous system before you begin.

3. Name what you're ready to release. On your paper, write down the patterns, identities, emotions, or memories that you sense are ready to be let go. Phrase each one as a clear statement of release:

> *I release the belief that I must earn the right to rest.*
>
> *I release the shame and embarrassment I carry from this memory.*
>
> *I release the need to play the martyr in my relationships.*
>
> *I release the pattern of gossip that drains my energy.*

As you write, pause to notice what sensations might arise in your body, like tightness, warmth, or release. Each one is a signal of something shifting.

4. Speak your releases aloud. When you are ready, read each statement slowly, allowing emotion to move through you. Tears, laughter, or sighs are all ways your body completes the stress cycle.

5. Symbolically release. Choose a physical act that represents letting go: Burn your list safely, or tear it into pieces. Submerge it in water, or bury it in the earth.

6. Close your ritual. Take another deep breath and say, "I now make space for that which truly aligns with me."

Afterward, you may want to journal about how your body feels, what emotions surfaced, or what new energy you sense emerging. You might find that repeating this ritual seasonally, or whenever a chapter of life feels complete, creates a deeper sense of clarity, lightness, and safety within.

Journal Prompts

Notice

- When you imagine letting go of an old identity or role, what sensations arise in your body, for instance relief, fear, grief, expansion?

- When something doesn't go as planned, where does your mind go first: blame, self-criticism, or curiosity? How does your nervous system respond in each case?

- Do you notice any places where you might be waiting for someone else to change, apologize, or validate you before you allow yourself to move forward?

Reflect

- Can you trace one limiting belief back to a specific moment, person, or environment in your life? What did that belief once protect you from?

- What beliefs about yourself have quietly shifted from *I think* into *I am*? How do these beliefs live in your body?

- Are there areas of your life where you still feel stuck in an old story that no longer fits? What would it mean to gently loosen your grip on it?

Integrate

- Which limiting beliefs are you ready to release? Which new belief feels truer to who you are becoming?

- Are there any situations where you still hold someone else responsible for your current pain? If so, what might it look like to gently reclaim your power, not to excuse their actions, but to release the emotional hold they still have over you?

Rewiring Your Outlook

I am the author of my story.

Going Forward

Letting go of what no longer serves you is how you create space for a new story to emerge. Every time you release an old belief, identity, or limitation, you teach your nervous system that it is safe to expand beyond the patterns of the past. The narratives that once kept you small were never proof of your unworthiness, they were simply survival strategies. Now, as you shed those limiting beliefs, you make room for new truths to take root: that rest is allowed, that you are worthy without striving, and that safety and abundance can coexist.

Rewriting your story is not about erasing the past; it's about choosing, moment by moment, to align your present with who you are becoming.

This process does not instantly erase the inner voices shaped by years of survival; it simply gives you the awareness to meet them differently.

In the next chapter, we explore how your inner voice was formed, how it mirrors your nervous system states, and how to shift it from criticism to compassion. Here, you'll learn to speak to yourself in a way that builds safety, strengthens regulation, and supports the life you are designing. This chapter is where your new story becomes a lived experience, one gentle, intentional thought at a time.

CHAPTER 10

EMOTIONAL REPATTERNING & INNER DIALOGUE

Emotional repatterning is the process of gently rewiring how we experience, interpret, and respond to emotions. It is how we shift from being ruled by our emotional reactions to relating to them with awareness and compassion. It's not about control; it's about connection. When we can meet our emotions with presence rather than resistance, we create safety within the body.

The Observer Revisited

We explored emotional observation as part of rooting, but it deserves another look as we rise. Awareness is the foundation of all repatterning. When we pause to notice an emotion, we interrupt the chain reaction that would normally follow. That pause gives us enough space to respond instead of react.

Emotions are messengers. They show us what needs care and attention. The goal is not to suppress or fix them. They have to be acknowledged and observed, not denied or belittled.

Five Steps for Emotional Repatterning

1. Notice: Become aware of the feeling as it arises in the body.

2. Name: Label the emotion, not yourself (e.g., *I am feeling anxious*, not *I am anxious.*)

3. Acknowledge: Let it exist without judgment. Allow it to be there.

4. Explore: Ask with curiosity: "What is this emotion trying to tell me?"

5. Release: Breathe through it. Let it move through your system rather than clinging to it.

By catching the emotion, you stop the cycle of having emotional reactions to situations that are often hurtful and unproductive. Every time you do this, you show your body that it is safe to feel. And when you respond instead of react, you are choosing and acting from a more rational and grounded space.

Over time, emotional regulation stops being an act of control and becomes an act of trust. At first, regulation can feel like something you *have to actively do:* managing reactions, monitoring emotions, trying not to fall apart.

As safety takes root, something shifts. You stop trying to manage yourself into acceptable shapes and start listening instead. You trust your body's timing, your capacity, and your ability to return to center. You no longer need to clamp down on your feelings or push them away. Emotions no longer feel like threats to be contained, but information to be felt and integrated.

From this place, responses emerge naturally, not from fear of losing control, but from confidence in your inner steadiness. This is the shift that allows you to move through life with more ease, clarity, and self-trust, knowing that your body can move through emotion without being overwhelmed, and that even strong feelings will rise, crest, and pass. Regulation becomes less about restraint and more about a steady, compassionate presence with whatever arises.

Emotional Responsibility

People will often say things like, "You made me feel angry" or "You made me feel sad." Hearing the response, "I can't make you feel anything" can then feel really irritating. People can make you feel all kinds of emotions—can't they?

Believing that other people have control over our emotions can make us feel blindsided when someone "makes" us feel an emotion, and powerless to stop it. We were conditioned from a young age that our internal emotions were caused by external events, with phrases like, "they hurt my feelings" being commonplace. Then, when we are blame shifting our emotions, there is no room to explore why we felt the emotion in the first place because we are placing the cause of that emotion in someone else's hands.

What you are really doing is blaming someone else for your emotional reaction. In reality, no one can truly *make* you feel anything. Words and actions can stir old wounds, but how you respond belongs entirely to you. This realization is deeply empowering. When you take ownership of your emotions, you move from reaction to responsibility, and from victimhood to sovereignty.

The other side of that is you are not in control of or responsible for anyone else's emotions either. When someone says, "You made me feel bad," you can meet that statement with compassion without taking responsibility for their emotional state. It doesn't feel good to be blamed for something, but in the end, it is their emotion, not yours. What we can do is model what emotional awareness looks like by reframing. Instead of "You make me feel angry," it can sound like "I feel angry when you say that." That subtle shift keeps you connected to your own truth without giving your power away.

Relearning Emotional Validation

Have you ever had someone judge, dismiss, or criticize your emotions? This is emotional invalidation; our inner experience is dismissed or criticized. When this happens, we can experience shame around our feelings. If we have self-worth wounds, we may agree with that person, thinking that our emotions are not only unacceptable, but they are unimportant.

Many of us learned early on that our emotions were too much. We might have been told:

> *Calm down.*
>
> *Toughen up.*
>
> *Stop crying, you are fine.*
>
> *Stop getting upset.*
>
> *You have no right to be angry.*

These messages taught our nervous systems that expressing emotion was unsafe. When invalidation happens repeatedly, we internalize it. We silence our own feelings with thoughts like *I shouldn't feel this way* or *it's not that bad*. We suppress our emotions rather than observe and explore.

Healing begins with validation, giving yourself permission to feel and observe without judgment. It doesn't mean approving of what happened or enjoying what you feel. It means meeting the present moment honestly, without resistance. You might say to yourself:

> *Of course I feel sad right now. That was painful.*
>
> *Of course I feel angry. My boundaries were crossed.*

Validation creates space for safety. When your emotions are allowed to exist, your nervous system no longer needs to fight or defend against them. You start to rebuild internal trust, which is foundational to emotional regulation.

Affirmations & Brain Rewiring

Affirmations are not about pretending to feel something that you don't. They are gentle reminders of truths your body may have forgotten, and the repetition helps form new neural pathways that replace old limiting beliefs.

Start small and choose affirmations that feel believable:

> *I am learning to feel safe in my body.*
>
> *I am open to success.*
>
> *I am worthy of love and rest.*

Affirmations that are too far from your current reality may feel forced and unsafe. Begin where you are and expand from there. Over time, these words become part of your body's new language of calm and trust.

Nervous System Reset: Cultivating Everyday Safety & Support

You've begun to build a foundation of safety through awareness and basic self-care. Now, as your body learns to trust calm and consistency, we can gently expand those practices. These reset pathways are about bringing comfort, presence, and kindness into your daily rhythm. The small, consistent acts reinforce safety through experience rather than thought, and teach your nervous system that life can feel safe, steady, and even enjoyable.

The Practice

Look for small ways to weave safety into your life. Try these:

- Move your body daily. Even a few minutes of stretching, dancing, or walking can shift stagnant energy and signal vitality to your system.

- Engage your senses. Light a candle. Diffuse essential oils, or open a window for fresh air. These small sensory cues bring you back into the present moment and anchor your awareness in safety.

- Let music support your mood. Choose sounds that uplift, soothe, or inspire you.

- Nourish yourself with intention. Cook a meal slowly and mindfully. Try a new recipe and eat on your favorite plates. The act of preparing food with care reminds your body that it deserves nourishment, not urgency.

- Create a comfortable place to relax. Design a small space in your home where you can unwind. You can use pillows, a soft blanket, gentle lighting or whatever else feels right. Let it become your safe retreat.

- Practice kind self-talk. Say something encouraging to yourself every day, even if it feels awkward at first. Your body listens.

- Turn routines into rituals. Don't rush through your shower. Feel its warmth. Breathe in the steam, and remind yourself that you are cared for.

- Donate items that you no longer need. Clearing physical space can help clear emotional space, signaling your body that it's safe to let go.

- Share a hug or hold hands. Gentle, consensual touch calms the vagus nerve and deepens feelings of connection.

- Pet a dog or cat. This calms the nervous system, lowers cortisol, and releases oxytocin, which creates a sense of safety and connection.

- Complete a small task. Check something off your to-do list that you have been putting off. The momentum will build your confidence, and you'll release the stress attached to the lingering task.

Journal Prompts

Notice

- How do you feel when you assign responsibility for your emotions to others, for example, when you say, "You made me feel . . . "? Does that bring relief, frustration, or a sense of powerlessness?

- How does it feel in your body when someone dismisses or invalidates your emotions? What sensations or thoughts arise in that moment?

- Are there emotions that tend to linger longer in your body? What might they be asking for underneath, for instance, rest, boundaries, or understanding?

Reflect

- Are there emotions that you tend to express easily and others that you often suppress? What makes some emotions feel safer to show than others?

- Have you ever been made to feel responsible for someone else's emotions? What patterns do you notice? Does this happen with the same person, or around similar emotions?

- Can you think of any situations where you minimized or invalidated your own emotions? What was happening around you at the time?

Integrate

- What does emotional validation look or sound like to you? How can you offer this to yourself more consistently?

- What would it feel like to fully trust your emotions as guides rather than as problems to fix?

Rewiring Your Outlook

I can respond instead of react.

Going Forward

As you move forward, remember that emotional repatterning is not about controlling what you feel. It is about changing how you relate to it. Each time you notice an emotion, name it with honesty, and respond with compassion instead of judgment, you interrupt old survival loops and create new pathways of safety. This is how emotional responsibility becomes empowering rather than heavy: not through suppression, but through awareness and choice. Over time, your inner dialogue begins to shift, your nervous system learns that feelings are safe to experience, and your capacity to respond with clarity and steadiness grows.

As you deepen this relationship with your inner world, there may still be the quieter, more persistent voices that linger beneath the surface. They are whispers of not enough, too much, or unworthy that once shaped your choices and identity. These voices were never your truth; they were learned protections, echoes of environments where you had to earn love, safety, or belonging.

In the next chapter, we turn toward these internalized judgments with compassion and clarity. This chapter invites you to understand where the inner critic came from and how it has tried to keep you safe. Then we explore how to cultivate a new inner authority rooted in self-respect rather than self-doubt. Here, you will begin transforming the parts of you that once tore you down into parts that finally lift you up.

—

CHAPTER 11

HEALING THE INNER CRITIC & SELF-RESPECT WOUNDS

Your nervous system listens to every word you think and speak, and so your inner dialogue is shaping your reality. The way that you speak to yourself determines how safe you feel in your own body. When your inner voice is harsh or critical, your nervous system experiences it as a threat. Negative self-talk keeps your body in tension, and over time this creates a loop of self-judgment and stress.

Many of us inherited the voice of our inner critic from the people who raised or influenced us. If your parents, caregivers, or teachers dismissed emotions or demanded perfection, self-criticism likely became your inner language. Perhaps you had past experiences where you felt rejection or emotional harm. The inner critic is trying to protect you from external pain by self-inflicting it, preempting outside criticism by being the first to criticize. It is trying to keep you small to prevent perceived failure, and in doing so keeping the nervous system feeling safe as well.

We often talk to ourselves in a way that we would *never* use toward another person. This negative inner dialogue causes the body to tense, holding our nervous systems in a chronic state of dysregulation. We learned this voice from modeled behavior, generational patterns, and cultural conditioning. But now that we are aware, we can speak differently.

Changing your inner dialogue begins with awareness. Notice the way that you speak to yourself. You may hear things like *I should be doing more* or *I always mess things up*. Instead of brushing that thought aside, get curious. Who does that sound like? When did you start talking to yourself like that? Is there something that voice is trying to protect you from? Bringing compassion and understanding to your inner critic allows that voice to soften. You realize that perhaps those cruel thoughts represent parts of you that are trying to be seen.

Would you ever speak to your best friend, your child, or someone you love the way you speak to yourself? If the answer is no, change the dialogue. Start by asking: *Would I speak this way to someone I love?*

The nervous system softens when your inner voice becomes kind, as gentle self-talk signals safety. Instead of disappointment and shame, offer yourself grace and encouragement. Say things like:

It's okay. I'm still learning.

I did my best today.

I'm allowed to rest.

Nice try.

I've got this.

When you replace criticism with compassion, your body begins to relax. The nervous system learns that it is safe to make mistakes and to rest. Each time you offer yourself understanding instead of judgment, you rewire your emotional patterns toward self-trust and safety. Your inner voice is meant to hold space for you, not punish you. When you practice compassionate self-talk consistently, your nervous system can root into safety.

Learning to Feel Pride

I remember a situation where I came through in the heat of the moment and prevented an accident from occurring. I knew that I had saved the day so to speak, but when I told myself that I was proud of my actions and quick thinking, I felt uncomfortable. That small moment revealed how much work I still had to do learning to feel safe in feeling pride and restoring my self-worth.

For those of us that have dysregulated nervous systems, feeling proud of ourselves can feel strange and uncomfortable. We have learned to equate pride with danger or rejection, and so rather than celebrating ourselves, we dismiss, downplay, or perhaps even criticize.

As a result of our self-worth wounds, our inner critic wants to minimize achievements. We tell ourselves that we could have done better, or we pick out all of the things that went wrong instead of celebrating what went well.

Why is it so hard for us to feel proud of ourselves? This can be multifaceted. Maybe our achievements were ignored or minimized, so celebrating ourselves never felt natural. Having pride may have felt unsafe; having our accomplishments celebrated may have caused others to criticize or be jealous. Our bodies then equated pride with danger as we learned that we would get hurt if we shined. The inner critic steps in to shrink us back down: *Don't get too confident. Don't draw attention to yourself.* In some families or cultures, humility may have been a prized virtue and so any amount of pride felt wrong.

Many of us have learned to equate pride with arrogance. We've been told not to brag or "get a big head," but there is a profound difference between pride and arrogance.

Pride says: *I am proud of what I've done.*

Arrogance says: *I am better than you.*

How do we move past the discomfort of pride? We must learn to feel it safely. Start by celebrating small, low-stakes moments. Tell yourself that you are proud of what you accomplished, how you handled a situation, or how you showed up. Notice how it feels in your body. You don't have to say it in front of anyone else. When you are comfortable, try sharing your small wins with close friends and family.

This is nervous system work. And over time, pride becomes a bridge to a deeper worthiness. You are teaching your body that self-respect and celebration are safe. When you allow yourself to feel pride, you internalize love rather than needing to prove yourself and receive external validation.

The Martyr Wound

The martyr is someone who always says yes and puts others first. You sacrifice your needs, ignore your own boundaries, and sacrifice your happiness for the supposed happiness of others. Maybe you feel like you don't deserve to be happy, you are trying to avoid conflict, or you are falling into a people-pleasing role.

When you take on the martyr role, it is your nervous system trying to keep you safe or earn your worth. The martyr role is a survival strategy. *If I give enough, I'll be safe. If I sacrifice, I'll be loved.* But over time this will leave you feeling depleted, exhausted, and maybe even resentful. You become disconnected from your own needs because you think that they don't matter, and you are giving your body the message that your worth depends on how much you suffer.

Here are some signs that you take on the martyr role:

- You say *yes* when you want to say *no*.

- The idea of rest and relaxation makes you feel guilty.

- The thought of putting yourself first makes you feel guilty.

- You consistently give from an empty cup.

- You feel invisible even when doing things for others.

- Receiving feels selfish and uncomfortable.

Over time, this pattern leads to burnout and resentment. When reciprocity doesn't come, your inner critic lashes out: *You didn't do enough. You should have tried harder.*

Taking on the martyr role means that you are constantly over-extending yourself, and suppressing your needs eventually leads to burnout. Then, when you might be looking for reciprocity and it doesn't come, you feel resentful, and perhaps even trigger your inner critic because you feel like you did something wrong. You might feel like you need to give more to overcompensate, and the nervous system remains caught in a loop of over-giving and self-blame. Healing begins when you decide to honor your needs as valid and important.

Healing the Martyr Wound

- Recognize that your needs matter.

- Pause and check in with yourself before saying yes.

- Practice small boundaries: "I can't right now."

- Let someone help without rushing to repay it.

- Schedule guilt-free rest.

Remember, your light will shine brightest if it is lighting your own path first.

Trauma Bonds & Self-Respect

A trauma bond is an unhealthy attachment marked by periods of abuse or neglect mixed with periods of love and forgiveness. Even though you can see the bad parts, you still feel bonded to that person because they are still a source of love sometimes. There is often lots of intensity and drama, yet you feel unable to leave. You may believe that things will get better if you try a little harder, or that maybe this time things will be different.

Trauma bonds are rooted in unworthiness, believing that you are receiving what you deserve. As you heal your self-respect wounds, you realize that you deserve more. When you notice the trauma bond and the steps in the cycle, you can put up boundaries and replace the old patterns with new ones.

Reframing Negative Thought Patterns

Negative self-talk is very harmful, keeping the nervous system in a chronic state of alert. We do not feel safe in our bodies, and over time, this inner voice is mistaken for truth. But those stories are not facts. You can change your inner dialogue, looking upon yourself with grace and compassion. When you interrupt a negative thought and replace it with a kinder one, you are signaling to the body that it is safe. The nervous system learns that it no longer must brace for attack, and self-respect becomes your new story.

Nervous System Reset: Body Forgiveness Exercise

Our bodies often carry layers of shame, resentment, and disappointment that have quietly built up from years of self-criticism and comparison to others. The purpose of this practice is to heal your relationship with your body, to shift from judgment to gratitude and reconciliation. When we forgive the body for the ways we have neglected or criticized it, we begin rebuilding the foundation of self-respect from the inside out.

The Practice

1. Find a quiet and comfortable place where you can be alone for several minutes. Take a few deep breaths to ground yourself and find presence.

2. Gently scan your body, beginning with your toes. Ask yourself:

> *Have I spoken unkindly to this part of myself?*
>
> *Have I ignored or overworked it?*
>
> *Have I carried unrealistic expectations here?*

3. Notice where tension, shame, or discomfort live. Breathe deeply and allow any emotion that surfaces to move through you.

4. Speak these words of compassion and forgiveness, softly and deliberately:

> *I'm sorry.*
>
> *Please forgive me.*
>
> *Thank you.*
>
> *I love you.*

5. Continue scanning up your body: your toes, your feet, your legs, your belly, your hands, your shoulders, your face. Offer gratitude as you go. It can sound like this:

> *Thank you, legs, for carrying me through this life.*
>
> *Thank you, hands, for the ways you create and hold.*
>
> *Thank you, eyes, for allowing me to see this beautiful world.*

6. Thank your body for what it has carried, what it has performed, and for what it has survived. Thank your body for the joy it has allowed you to experience.

7. When you reach the end of your body scan, place both hands over your heart and take a deep breath. Whisper to yourself in closing: *Thank you. I love you.*

This sequence of words used above comes from hoʻoponopono, a traditional Hawaiian practice of reconciliation and forgiveness that means "to make right" or "to return to harmony." It was a family or community process facilitated by a healer or elder, where conflicts were openly discussed, forgiveness offered, and harmony restored among members.

The modern version of this practice, shared by Hawaiian healer Morrnah Simeona and later popularized by Dr. Ihaleakala Hew Len, uses the simple mantra: *"I'm sorry. Please forgive me. Thank you. I love you."* It is a way to cleanse memories, release emotional burdens, and restore inner peace.

The four statements represent a cycle of emotional and energetic reconciliation:

- "I'm sorry" acknowledges responsibility or awareness of pain.

- "Please forgive me" opens the door to compassion.

- "Thank you" expresses gratitude for the opportunity to release.

- "I love you" restores connection and balance within oneself and others.

When spoken with presence, these words become a nervous system reset, softening the body, signaling safety, and allowing old emotional residue to dissolve with grace.

Journal Prompts

Notice

- What does self-respect mean to you right now? How does it feel in your body when you act from a place of self-respect versus self-sacrifice?

- When someone offers you praise or recognition, how does your body respond? Do you tense up or minimize the praise, or can you receive it openly?

- How comfortable are you with the idea of feeling proud of yourself? When you tell yourself, *I'm proud of you*, what sensations arise in the body?

Reflect

- Can you remember when you first started hearing your inner critic? Do you recall an experience or relationship where this voice began to form? (It's okay if you don't remember.)

- What do you judge about yourself most often? Is it your voice that you are hearing or someone else's?

- When you think of something your inner critic has said recently, what do you think that voice is trying to protect you from?

Integrate

- How do you usually speak to yourself when you make a mistake? What might it sound like to respond to yourself with compassion instead of criticism?

- Is there a recent accomplishment, big or small, that you have not fully acknowledged yet? How could you pause to celebrate? What emotions arise when you try to celebrate something you've done well?

Rewiring Your Outlook

I honor my needs with compassion.

Going Forward

As you continue this work, remember that healing your inner critic is not about silencing it completely, it is about transforming that voice into one of compassion, guidance, and safety. When you meet your self-judgment with empathy, you teach your body that it no longer needs to brace for impact. Each time you choose to celebrate yourself rather than diminish your worth, you strengthen your foundation of self-respect.

This is the heart of nervous system healing: replacing fear-based patterns with trust-based awareness. The more you speak to yourself with kindness, the more your body learns that it is safe to rest, to receive, and to take up space.

In the next chapter, we'll explore how this inner safety expands outward. Honoring your limits, needs, and energy through healthy boundaries becomes a living expression of self-respect. They protect your peace, preserve your energy, and allow your nervous system to feel safe in connection.

—

CHAPTER 12

BOUNDARIES AS A NERVOUS SYSTEM PRACTICE

Self-abandonment happens when we disconnect from our own needs, limits, and inner signals in order to maintain harmony, avoid conflict, or earn belonging. It is a learned nervous system strategy. When the body senses that expressing a need or setting a boundary might jeopardize connection, it chooses to stay quiet, shrink, please, or over-function. In the moment, we are surviving, but over time, self-abandonment erodes trust in ourselves. We stop believing our emotions matter. We override our intuition, and we move through the world as if the comfort of others is more important than our own truth. Healing this pattern begins with noticing those micro-moments when we say *yes* while our body says *no*, when we dismiss our feelings, or when we make ourselves small to keep the peace.

Boundaries Are Bridges

Boundaries are not walls. They are bridges to self-respect, energy regulation, and nervous system safety. Healthy boundaries do not separate us from the world; rather, they help us meet it from a place of grounded authenticity.

We often hear that we should say *yes* more—yes to opportunities, yes to more experiences, and yes to new beginnings. But equally powerful is the ability to say *no*. Saying no is not rejection or withdrawal; it is an act of clarity and self-trust. You are telling your nervous system: *I am listening to you. I am honoring your limits*.

When I first entered this part of my nervous system healing journey, I noticed that I stopped wanting to make plans. I became more spontaneous, honoring how I felt in the moment rather than filling my calendar out of obligation. This was a huge shift for me. For years, my planner had been an extension of my identity, where plans were made ahead of time and followed through with, out of a sense of obligation. I did not want to seem like I was flaking out on someone, so I would push through plans that I had made at the expense of my nervous system.

I began to realize that keeping commitments that I probably should have said no to in the first place just to appear dependable was often a form of self-betrayal. To avoid these situations, I became more discerning when I made plans. I realized that I could honor my desire to be reliable to friends and family *and* honor my own needs at the same time.

Now, I still make plans, but I also make room for my nervous system's needs. If I need rest, quiet, or space, I feel comfortable taking it. That might mean saying, "I don't really want to do that," and trusting that honesty creates more authentic relationships.

It is impossible to make everyone happy all the time, and it's not our job to "make" anyone feel anything. Happiness is, after all, an inside job. When we live from this understanding, guilt loosens its grip. It is okay to not feel like pushing through commitments all the time, and we do not owe explanations for our need to rest either.

As I began setting boundaries, I went through a phase of saying *no* a lot, maybe even overcompensating for years of people-pleasing. It felt powerful, even healing, to protect my own energy for once. I stayed home more often and started tuning in to how different people, events, and environments were affecting my energy and vibration. Checking in with my inner compass offered clarity on how I felt about different situations. Gradually, I released the guilt of disappointing others. When you honor your limits, some people may respond with frustration, disappointment, or even anger, but remember that those reactions belong to them, not to you.

Healthy boundaries are not about control. They are a wonderful way of showing yourself love and respect, and they can help you embody a sense of confidence. They teach others how to meet you while also showing your nervous system that it is safe to rest, to say no, and to take up space.

Having boundaries also allows us to develop relationships rooted in mutual respect. It may feel difficult the first few times you establish boundaries, but it does get easier. Stepping away from people-pleasing in this way is another step toward nervous system wealth. Establishing and sticking to firm boundaries, while also allowing for preference flexibility, is the ultimate form of self-respect.

Additional Types of Boundaries

Emotional Boundaries

Emotional boundaries protect your inner landscape. They separate what feelings are yours to hold and what belongs to others. When you take on the emotions of others as your own, your nervous system absorbs their energy and stays in a state of alertness. Emotional boundaries remind your body that you can care deeply without carrying everything. You can be compassionate without absorbing. You can witness another's pain yet also remain grounded in your own center.

Communication Boundaries

Communication boundaries define how you engage in conversations, especially when tension or conflict arises. They can sound like, "I'm not available for this conversation right now," or "I need a moment before I respond." These simple statements give your body the space it needs to respond instead of react. Communication boundaries are nervous system tools that make dialogue feel more safe, calm, and intentional.

Relational Boundaries

These help to shape the structure and reciprocity of your relationships with family, friendships, work, and love. They ask: *Is there balance here? Is there mutual respect?* Healthy relationships thrive on reciprocity. Relationships that are one-sided are depleting. You should not have to lose yourself to stay connected.

Mental Boundaries

Mental boundaries protect your thoughts, beliefs, and perspectives. They allow you to hold your own truth without internalizing the opinions or projections of others. When you feel that you must constantly justify or defend yourself, your body perceives that as emotional threat. You don't need to prove your worth or convince anyone of your perspective. You knowing your own truth is enough.

Physical Boundaries

Physical boundaries protect your personal space, your body, and your sensory environment. This includes how close others stand to you, if touch feels comfortable, and how much time alone you need. Your nervous system can relax when it knows your body feels safe. If certain environments feel overstimulating, it is perfectly okay to step away or take a few minutes of solitude without feeling guilt.

Financial & Energetic Boundaries

Energetic boundaries involve how you exchange your time and resources. This is something to be especially mindful of if you are a caregiver, healer, or creative. Undercharging, over-giving, or saying *yes* to unpaid emotional labor teaches your nervous system scarcity and exhaustion. Healthy exchange teaches your body that abundance and generosity can coexist with self-respect. You are allowed to receive as much as you give.

Practicing & Embodying Boundaries

If you are used to people-pleasing, then boundary setting can feel selfish at first. You may worry about letting someone down, or you may be afraid of rejection. But when you consistently say yes at your own expense, you teach your body that your needs don't matter. Over time, that message becomes internalized as chronic stress, resentment, or burnout.

Boundaries are a somatic practice. When you tune in to your body, you notice that your body is already giving you clues about what boundaries it needs, and about what feels safe and nourishing versus scary and intrusive. You might feel tightness in your chest when something feels wrong, or a soft, expansive sense of calm when something feels right. This is your body reacting before you even consciously think about it.

Start practicing boundaries gently:

- Notice what feels off, draining, or unsafe.

- Allow yourself to pause or delay a response: "Let me get back to you."

- Practice setting boundaries in low-stakes situations to build nervous system safety.

- Reframe the inner critic that calls boundaries "selfish." Boundaries are sacred. They are a deep form of self-love.

Boundaries are not rigid; they can hold flexibility. You can compromise on preferences while standing firm on core needs. For example, you might agree to change plans with a friend but still hold firm on your time limit because rest is nonnegotiable.

You don't owe anyone detailed explanations for your boundaries. Overexplaining often invites negotiation. You can stand firm with simple statements:

> *That doesn't work for me.*
>
> *I can't commit to that right now.*
>
> *I'm not available for that conversation.*
>
> *I need some time before I decide.*

When we learn to tune in to our inner system of yes and no, and we speak and act from that place, we grow in self-awareness and in turn our self-respect. Each time you protect your peace, you're retraining your nervous system to recognize that safety comes from honoring yourself.

- You are allowed to say no.
- You are allowed to change your mind.
- You are allowed to rest.

And you are worthy of relationships that honor that truth.

Safe Vulnerability

As we heal the nervous system, we become more rooted in safety, and then vulnerability becomes possible. When the body is no longer bracing for danger, we naturally soften. The walls we once built for survival feel less necessary, and we become willing to let others see more of who we truly are.

When the nervous system is in a sympathetic state, vulnerability feels threatening. The body remembers moments of past rejection, shame, or criticism, and so opening up and sharing deep parts of ourselves can feel dangerous. Sharing our truth, admitting our needs, or allowing ourselves to be seen can feel risky because those old wounds taught us that exposure leads to hurt.

But vulnerability is not the absence of boundaries. As we strengthen our sense of worthiness and safety, we can share from grounded authenticity. Then vulnerability becomes a way of creating real connection, informed by trust, self-respect, and nervous system safety.

Vulnerability can also show up in small, everyday moments. For me, I began noticing healing when I could laugh at myself without feeling the sting of shame and when I could make a mistake and not spiral into self-judgment. These were signs that my self-worth wounds were softening.

Safe vulnerability is not about sharing everything with everyone, as some may not be deserving of your inner world. Part of boundary work is discerning where your vulnerability will be held with care and where it will not. You owe no one access to the deep parts of you unless your body senses safety there.

Nervous System Reset: Decluttering Exercise

Clutter is more than a visual inconvenience. When we allow our physical space to become cluttered, we can trigger stress responses in the body. A crowded, disorganized space sends subtle danger cues to the brain, signaling unfinished tasks, unresolved decisions, and a lack of order. Clutter feels noisy and chaotic. This can activate stress hormones and make it difficult for the body to relax and unwind.

Decluttering goes beyond just tidying. A more orderly environment can bring about a visual sense of peace and spaciousness. This, in turn, can help bring the nervous system back into a state of calm. Even small shifts can significantly impact how grounded and safe we feel in our own home.

There are many different strategies and ways to declutter. Entire books and websites are devoted to the topic, offering various systems and philosophies. If it feels possible, allow yourself to reach a natural sense of completion, even if the space isn't perfect. Finishing the small area offers your nervous system the reward of completing a task. Try approaching it as a ritual of reset rather than a chore, maybe listening to fun music as you go. If decluttering feels supportive to you, and your body wants a little structure, you might take this practice further.

The Practice

1. Choose one small area that feels manageable. You might pick a junk drawer, a shelf, one corner of a room, a nightstand, or the top of your desk. Another method is setting a timer for fifteen to thirty minutes and stopping when the timer ends, leaving enough time to put everything away again.

2. Empty the space completely. Place items into piles: keep, donate, trash, and unsure. Don't pressure yourself to make every decision as you can revisit the unsure pile later.

3. Clean the empty space with intention. Wipe surfaces slowly and consciously. Imagine stagnant, heavy energy moving out of the space, perhaps even opening a window to let some fresh air in.

4. Put back in an orderly fashion what you have decided to keep. Organize in a way that feels soothing and supportive.

5. Follow through with donations and trash removal. Completion sends a powerful signal of capability and safety to your nervous system.

6. Pause and notice. Take a moment to observe how you feel after taking the time to clean, declutter, and organize different spaces in your home.

Journal Prompts

Notice

- How do you feel when you sense that a boundary is needed but you are unable to set it? When you imagine finally setting a boundary that you have long avoided, how do you feel? Relieved? Anxious? Empowered?

- Are there people or situations in your life where vulnerability feels safe and welcome? Where in your life does vulnerability feel unsafe? How does your body feel in each case?

- Are there places in your life where you are ignoring your own boundaries, even when you know what you need? How do you feel when you do this?

Reflect

- Where in your life have you learned to prioritize harmony over honesty?

- What boundaries are you afraid to set because you fear losing someone's approval, love, or acceptance?

- Where in your life do you tend to overextend yourself? What are you hoping will happen by doing so? What fear lies underneath?

Integrate

- If your body had the final say in what you allow or accept, what would it tell you to stop tolerating?

- Imagine yourself living with strong, healthy boundaries. How do you move through the world differently? How do you speak, rest, love, work?

Rewiring Your Outlook

*I am worthy of boundaries
that protect my nervous system.*

Going Forward

As you honor your needs with clearer boundaries, your nervous system learns a new pattern: that safety can come from self-respect. Each time you stand firm in your boundaries, you add to a powerful foundation of internal trust. Over time, these small, consistent acts of boundary setting shift how you experience yourself in the world, from bracing against it to standing securely within it.

In the next chapter, we build upon this inner safety. Instead of shaping your life from old wounds or external expectations, you'll learn to design your choices, desires, and direction from the grounded wisdom of your body. You are no longer living from survival; you are learning to live from alignment.

—

CHAPTER 13

DESIGNING FROM
ROOTED WORTHINESS

Slowing down is not laziness; it is wisdom. It allows you to tune in to your intuition and disrupt old patterns. We no longer need to design our lives while disconnected from our bodies, building from old stories, inherited expectations, and long-established coping mechanisms. We no longer need strive toward someone else's definition of success, or paths chosen for us rather than by us, such as getting a "respectable" job, living a certain lifestyle, or stepping into roles and milestones before you feel ready.

When you design your life from your body rather than from old programs, everything shifts. You stop reacting to life. You take an active role instead of being passive and letting life happen to you. A grounded nervous system becomes the soil for authentic direction. You can create your reality with intention. You become attuned to the signals within by listening, trusting, and then aligning. Your choices become clearer, and you hold your boundaries more firmly. You stop pushing and instead pause to reflect. When you root into your truth, you will naturally choose what most aligns with you.

Designing From Regulation

Here are some signs that you are designing from a regulated nervous system state:

- You feel calm and steady in making decisions, even when faced with big decisions.

- You create without urgency or panic.

- You feel clarity in your thoughts.

- You honor your capacity instead of overriding it.

- You can sense the difference between desire and impulse.

- You are no longer motivated by receiving approval or external validation.

You may recognize some of these signs already. Others may still feel just out of reach. If you don't see yourself fully reflected here yet, that's okay. That may simply mean your nervous system is still learning what safety feels like.

When your body is stuck in survival mode, even your dreams can feel heavy. Your mind may want growth, but your nervous system isn't ready. As healing unfolds, your body can better flow between effort and rest. You stop fighting the current, getting things done from fear-based urgency and panic, or staying busy just to feel worthy. Your goals and desires become attuned to who you really are. Your nervous system is no longer a barrier to your vision, and that shift becomes the foundation for sustainable growth.

Worthiness Is a State

Worthiness is not something that we must achieve. It is not earned only to be lost if we fall short. When worthiness feels conditional, we fall into the loop of chasing approval. We measure ourselves through appearance, productivity, and performance. Even when we do succeed, satisfaction is short-lived because the nervous system is already bracing for the next moment that we fear not being enough. And so, we do not rest or slow down, and we postpone our joy until we reach a state of perfection, which we never do. This is how people become trapped in a cycle of endless striving.

To step out of this loop, the body must learn that it is safe to *be* without constantly proving ourselves. When you stop needing external validation, then your internal sense of belonging can grow. You realize that worthiness is a state of being, an inner steadiness and knowing. You accept yourself rather than looking for approval. You stop binding your self-worth to your appearance, performance, and productivity, and you value yourself for being exactly how you are right now.

You shift to a place of embodied worthiness with a deep knowing that you are already enough. You are already worthy. You always were.

The Four Feel-Good Neurochemicals

Our bodies are wired with four key neurochemicals: oxytocin, dopamine, serotonin, and endorphins. They can each powerfully influence our moods, motivation, sense of connection, and overall resilience. When we understand how these chemicals work, we can notice the negative behaviors that we exhibit in pursuit of these chemicals and shift toward more positive behaviors that have a more lasting, nourishing effect on our nervous system, rather than a quick fix that leaves us feeling depleted.

Oxytocin: The Love, Bonding & Connection Hormone

Unhealthy ways we chase it: people-pleasing; over-accommodating; tolerating poor boundaries in the hope of belonging

Healthy ways to support it: hugging; spending quality time with people we feel safe with; acts of kindness; petting animals; genuine emotional connection

Dopamine: The Reward & Motivation Signal

Unhealthy ways we chase it: compulsive scrolling; gambling; binge eating; impulse shopping

Healthy ways to support it: movement and exercise; setting achievable goals; completing tasks; learning something new; celebrating small wins

Serotonin: The Mood Stabilizer

Unhealthy ways we chase it: substances; micromanaging people or environments to feel in control

Healthy ways to support it: sunlight; healthy and nourishing food; consistent sleep; gratitude practice; meditation; spending time in nature

Endorphins: The Body's Relief & Euphoria Response

Unhealthy ways we chase it: over-exercising; thrill-seeking; pushing ourselves past exhaustion

Healthy ways to support it: laughter; dancing; singing; mindful exercise; deep breathing; creative flow

When we become aware of which chemicals we are chasing and how, we can shift from quick fixes to habits that regulate, support, and replenish the nervous system. This moves us out of survival patterns and into choices that feel nourishing, grounded, and aligned.

Practices for Shifting from a State of Proving to a State of Being

These practices help retrain your nervous system to settle into worthiness rather than chase it:

Regulate Through the Body

- Take a micro-moment. Pause, feel your feet on the ground, and tell yourself: *I am enough.*

- Ask your body what it needs before pushing through. Do you need a stretch break, some water, or perhaps a few moments of rest?

- Pause before committing. If someone asks something of you, take a breath before responding, taking notice of how your body feels.

Shift the Mindset

- Notice where your self-worth is conditional. For example*: If I lose weight, then I'll be happy. When I make more money, then I can rest.*

- Relax your grip on urgency. If something doesn't need to be done right now and you feel like you need to take a break, then honor that. This is not about avoidance. It is about honoring your capacity.

- Make a decision based on desire rather than expectations. Think about what you truly want, not what you think is expected of you.

Practice Safe Receiving

- Schedule rest and relaxation into your day without earning it. Teach your body that it is safe to rest.

- Receive without apologizing, downplaying, or reciprocating. For example, if someone offers you a compliment, just let it land, and take notice of any urge to deflect.

- Practice unproductive presence. Take a few minutes and do absolutely nothing, including no phone scrolling. Show your body that it is safe to just be.

The Pace of the World & the Nervous System

Life in our modern culture has accelerated. We champion speed and convenience. We live in a world of instant connection, instant information, and instant stimulation, but our nervous systems weren't built for this constant acceleration. We are overstimulated and restless. In a world where we can digitally connect instantly with people from anywhere in the world, we are more disconnected from real community than ever before.

When our bodies become used to being overstimulated, it can be difficult to relax and unwind. Slowing down feels foreign and uncomfortable while restlessness becomes what is familiar. Our phones are constantly going off with different notifications, and even our "relaxation" often includes constant scrolling. Instant access has blurred boundaries. Work emails, news, and messages are available all the time, and we are often expected to give quick responses.

This is all keeping our bodies in a state of heightened alertness. When we do not allow our nervous systems to go into rest and relax mode, we are keeping our bodies in a subtle fight-or-flight state. Slowing down in our world can feel like an act of rebellion, yet it is necessary for our nervous systems to heal. True rest requires intentionality, creating space, and reclaiming your bandwidth. When you learn to slow your pace and honor your capacity, your nervous system begins to trust you, and your life becomes something you design, not something you survive.

Nervous System Reset: The Five Senses Grounding Exercise

We can help the body return to presence when we anchor ourselves into the five senses. By engaging sight, sound, touch, taste, and smell, we signal to the nervous system that it can stop scanning for threats and settle into the safety of the present moment. This simple sensory scan reconnects the mind and body and creates an immediate sense of peace.

This practice is quick, accessible, and can be done anywhere. Use it whenever you feel like you need to quiet your mind, interrupt a spiral, and find presence again.

The Practice

1. Take a few slow, intentional breaths. Let your eyes soften as you take in the space around you.

2. Move through your senses one by one.

- Name five things you can see: Be specific, taking notice of colors, shapes, shadows, movement, or texture.

- Name four things you can hear: Listen for sounds both nearby and far away, obvious and subtle.

- Name three things you can feel: Tune in to things like texture, temperature, weight, and the sensations of clothing.

- Name two things you can smell: Notice scents like tea, fresh laundry, rain, a candle, or the air itself.

- Name one thing you can taste: Focus on the flavor of water, coffee, toothpaste, or even the taste of the air.

3. Now notice how you feel and what has shifted.

You will likely realize that the racing thoughts that you had before this practice feel softer or farther away. Your attention is no longer focused on future worries or memories of the past. You are simply present. You may feel curious or like you are noticing familiar surroundings for the first time.

Reflect on your practice. Was there one sense that was easier to connect to than others? Did you notice any one sense that felt more intense than the others?

Journal Prompts

Notice

- How long can you go without checking your phone notifications, news, email, texts, or social media? Do you feel obligated to answer messages and emails immediately? What might happen if you didn't?

- What cues does your body give you when it is nearing capacity or overwhelm?

- When you imagine simply being rather than constantly doing, how does your body respond? Does it welcome the stillness, or does it feel uncomfortable?

Reflect

- Were there times in your life when you felt you had to prove yourself to belong? Is that still true for you today? When you imagine designing your life from desire instead of expectation, what feels possible?

- Do you judge yourself when you want to rest or relax? What narratives arise when you slow down?

- Where in your life have you become accustomed to or dependent on instant access? How has this impacted your nervous system, relationships, or well-being?

Integrate

- What habits in your life chase the four feel-good neuro-chemicals in ways that don't fully support you? Are there healthier habits that would align more deeply with the life you want to build? How could you weave those habits into your daily life?

- What is one small way you could honor your body's need for rest this week, even if guilt arises?

Rewiring Your Outlook

My worth is inherent.

Going Forward

As you design your life from the grounded intelligence of your body, you step into a new kind of authorship. You are no longer shaping your life from urgency or self-doubt, but from alignment, truth, and worthiness. Designing from regulation means your decisions arise from clarity instead of fear, from intuition instead of pressure, from the present moment rather than past conditioning.

This chapter invited you to slow down long enough to hear the quiet wisdom within you, to recognize where your self-worth has been shaped by proving and performing, and to choose a more compassionate pace. As you root into embodied worthiness, life becomes something you intentionally create rather than something you struggle to keep up with.

As you design from this new grounded place, the world around you will not always move at the same pace. Others may still operate from urgency, chaos, or emotional reactivity. Their storms may try to pull you back into old patterns of over-functioning, absorbing, fixing, or responding before you've had a chance to breathe.

In the next chapter, we explore how to stay centered in the face of this external turbulence. You will learn how to recognize the hooks that pull you into drama, how to maintain emotional neutrality without disconnecting, and how to protect your peace without abandoning your compassion.

If Chapter 13 helped you anchor into your internal compass, Chapter 14 teaches you how to keep that compass steady, even when the winds around you begin to shift.

—

NOT REACTING TO DRAMA:
The Power of Peace

Drama thrives on reaction, quick responses, emotions, defensiveness, and subtle shifts in body language. When we get swept up in someone else's chaos, we allow their storm to disturb our peace. We internalize their emotions such as anger, fear, or frustration as our own, and our nervous systems absorb the impact. Learning to not react to storms that are not yours is an act of self-preservation, nervous system protection, and energetic sovereignty. It is not coldness or indifference. You are simply choosing not to carry what is not yours.

When you learn how to stand steady, you can hold onto your peace even while others are unsettled. You can stay centered while someone else spirals and listen without being swayed. You can choose responses that are aligned with your values instead of reacting from old wounds or triggers.

Emotional drama hooks you into a reactive state. These hooks often tap into past experiences of threat, so your body may respond before your mind has had a chance to access the situation. We get pulled into drama through gossip, accusations, "urgent" situations that are not truly urgent, passive-aggressive comments, unspoken expectations, triangulation, and personal attacks.

These hooks are designed, consciously or not, to provoke a nervous system reaction. The key to avoiding them is learning to pause, which gives your body time to regulate. The pause is where your power is. It gives you a chance to discern how or if you want to engage in the situation. You cannot control other people, but you can control how you respond.

When you pause before responding, you create space for clarity, regulation, and rational thought. By protecting your peace, you protect your self-worth, your energy, and your emotional vibration, which we cover more of in an upcoming chapter. Your peace is not to be given away.

Four Practices to Stay Centered in the Face of Drama

1. Remind yourself, *This is not mine*. This will signal to your nervous system that you are separating your emotional state from theirs.

2. Take two slow, intentional breaths before responding. This prevents urgency and reactivity from taking over.

3. Become the observer. Visualize stepping onto a balcony and watching the situation from above. Distance brings clarity, and this may allow you to see the whole picture and make a more informed decision.

4. State a boundary when needed. For example: "I'm not available to talk about this right now. Let's revisit it when we've both had a chance to calm down." Boundaries create space for regulation.

As you choose centered stillness over reactivity, you may notice certain people drift away, particularly those that have become addicted to drama.

Why People Become Addicted to Drama

What we label as a dramatic personality trait is frequently a nervous system adaptation, not a character flaw. People who seem to be constantly involved in drama may have grown up in a chaotic environment, and so peace may feel boring or even uncomfortable. If stressful environments are what our nervous systems are used to, then we will likely welcome the spikes in adrenaline and cortisol that drama can bring, perhaps even finding comfort in it. Drama becomes a way to regulate uncomfortable internal states or to feel momentarily important, connected, or energized.

There are also brain chemicals at work here. Drama can trigger a burst of dopamine, making the cycle feel rewarding, even if the aftermath is draining. That is perhaps why people seem to stay in cycles of drama. Breaking the drama cycle requires awareness, replacing drama-induced dopamine with healthy habits, and creating distance from people or situations that continually expose you. When you understand this, your body can soften. You no longer need to explain, fix, or absorb, you can simply stay steady.

Compassion Without Absorption

Choosing peace does not mean that you are dismissing, minimizing, or invalidating someone else's experience. It means that you are choosing not to absorb it by not getting emotionally involved. You can care without carrying the emotion.

Having compassion does not mean that we tolerate harmful behavior or soften boundaries for others. Rather, it is understanding that the behaviors of others often have little or nothing to do with you. Most people are speaking and acting from their own wounds, patterns, and triggers.

When you embody compassion, you stop taking things so personally. You recognize that someone's harsh tone, defensiveness, or emotional intensity may be rooted in their own nervous system dysregulation. With this awareness, you begin to understand, *This really isn't about me*, and your body stops bracing for attack. Then you can shift out of fight or flight, knowing that you do not need to defend, justify, or prove yourself.

When we no longer take the words and actions of others as personal attacks, we open the path to peace for our nervous system. Compassion softens the edges of conflict. And since our body no longer feels the need to react, we naturally lower our stress hormones. Compassion allows you to stay connected to your truth, no longer taking the projection of pain, fear, or anger from others personally, being pulled into someone else's emotional landscape. It is worth noting here that it may feel easier to show compassion for others once you've learned how to offer it to yourself.

Emotional Dumping

Some individuals rely on the energy of others as an emotional dumping ground, leaving you feeling exhausted, anxious, or drained. Their relief comes at your expense, and that imbalance becomes more obvious as you root deeper into your peace.

Emotional dumping happens when someone unloads their unprocessed emotions onto another person without consent, awareness, or regard for the impact it has on the listener. This is different from healthy emotional sharing. Sharing is mutual, intentional, and grounded in connection. Dumping is one-sided and often leaves you feeling drained and overwhelmed.

People often dump when their nervous system is dysregulated and they are seeking quick relief. Instead of processing their emotions as the observer or with appropriate support, they externalize the intensity onto someone else. Emotional dumping might look like urgent venting, catastrophizing, rehashing the same distress repeatedly, or projecting strong emotions such as anger or fear onto you. Sometimes these emotional dumping sessions are completely unexpected and catch you off guard. At other times they can be anticipated, as emotional dumping is often a repeated pattern.

You can care about someone deeply without absorbing their emotional overflow. Choosing not to carry their intensity is a necessary boundary for your own peace. You can listen with presence while staying grounded in your own body. You can be compassionate without allowing their nervous system dysregulation to hijack yours. A key part of protecting your peace is recognizing when someone is trying to push their emotions onto you and gently choosing not to take them on. You can remind yourself: *This is not mine.*

Making Assumptions

Assumptions are stories we create in our minds to fill in the gaps of missing information. These stories are shaped by past wounds, old patterns, habits, and the emotional lens through which we are currently viewing life. When we feel grounded and resourced, looking through a lens of positive emotion, our assumptions tend to be gentle and positive as well. When we feel stressed or insecure, looking through a negative lens, our assumptions become more negative, often turning neutral situations into imagined threats.

For example, if you text a friend and they don't reply right away, you might worry that you upset them or said the wrong thing, depending on what frame of mind you are in. You have assumed all the wrong things. Then your nervous system reacts as if your assumption is true, causing unnecessary suffering in the process, when in reality nothing is wrong, and the reason that they have not responded yet has nothing to do with you.

Assumptions can also distort how we interpret tone or inflection in messages. The same sentence can be read dozens of ways depending on your mood, and emphasizing different words can completely change how a sentence comes across. You believe you know how the message was meant to come across, but you may be projecting your own emotions onto their words.

At times, assumptions become hurtful judgments, stemming from jealousy or your own lack of self-worth. You may imagine someone else's life is "perfect," when we actually have no idea what they might be going through.

Why do we make assumptions? Uncertainty feels threatening, and so the mind fills in the blanks, even if the stories that we come up with are much more negative than the actual reality of the situation, just to avoid not knowing. Trust that you don't need all the answers. The unknown does not have to be dangerous.

Assumptions create drama, conflict, and misunderstanding, causing inner turmoil and unnecessary suffering. They can activate the nervous system just as strongly as real danger. Imagine that you walk into a room and a couple of people start to laugh. You assume that they must be laughing at you, and so your nervous system responds, and your body constricts. You feel embarrassed, wanting to melt into the floor. You wonder what about you is so funny. In reality, they are not laughing at you at all. You have only hurt yourself and caused unnecessary suffering by making assumptions.

Nervous System Reset: Laughter

Laughter can be a powerful somatic tool for resetting the nervous system. It shifts the body out of fight or flight, dissolving the emotional armor that we build to keep ourselves feeling safe. Laughter softens the tension we didn't realize we were carrying and reminds us that life does not need to feel so heavy and serious. It allows us to release stress while reconnecting us with the playfulness and joy of life.

It is interesting to note here that the body does not differentiate between genuine, spontaneous laughter and intentional, "fake" laughter. Both activate similar nervous system pathways, and often intentional laughter naturally turns real once your body gets going.

Laughter shifts the nervous system by activating a parasympathetic state. The physical contractions release stored tension and can discharge stress hormones. In addition, laughter with others provides social safety cues, strengthening feelings of connection and belonging.

The Science Behind It: Physical Benefits of Laughter

- Reduces stress hormones
- Boosts immune function
- Releases endorphins
- Elevates dopamine and serotonin
- Helps process and release pent-up emotion
- Improves blood flow

The Practice

Here are some gentle ways to invite more laughter into your daily life:

- Watch a funny video, show, or movie.

- Recall a silly memory and allow yourself to step back into the moment to relive the humor.

- Share jokes or funny stories with someone you feel comfortable with. (My husband has a daily dad-joke calendar that the kids love reading with him.)

Afterward, pause and reflect: Does your body feel lighter? Do you notice a shift in mood or energy? Is there someone in your life that you can naturally enjoy more laughter with?

Journal Prompts

Notice

- Recall a time when you reacted quickly to drama. How did that reaction feel in your body? Now imagine that same situation with a pause, responding instead of reacting. How does the outcome shift? How does your body feel in that version?

- Do you often take words or actions personally? Do you get defensive in those situations? How does that feel in your body?

- How does your body feel when you choose peace instead of engagement? What sensations signal regulation or relief?

Reflect

- Is there an area of your life where compassion for yourself or others feels difficult?

- In what areas of your life do you feel most pulled into drama? Is it linked to a specific person or environment? What makes the hook so strong?

- What does compassion without absorption feel like in your body? How is it different from fixing, rescuing, or carrying someone else's emotions?

Integrate

- What would it mean for you to treat your peace as something sacred rather than negotiable?

- What is one small way you could practice choosing stillness or peace instead of engagement this week?

Rewiring Your Outlook

I choose calm over chaos.

Going Forward

Peace is not something you wait for. It is something you practice. Each time you pause before reacting, each time you choose compassion over assumption, each moment you refuse to take on storms that are not yours, you strengthen the pathways to peace within yourself. You are teaching your nervous system that you can remain anchored even when the world around you is unsteady.

Going forward, let your inner calm be the place you return to, and remember that you do not need to absorb chaos to show that you care. The more you honor your peace, the more grounded and aligned you will feel.

As you anchor yourself in peace, a new layer of energy awareness naturally emerges. Just as you learned to recognize emotional hooks and drama spirals, you will now notice where your energy is being drained, where you feel depleted, and where your nervous system struggles to stay grounded.

The next chapter invites you to explore what it means to protect your energy as a sacred resource. You will learn how to stay resourced from within, how to recognize energetic leaks, and how to create a life that supports your vitality instead of pulling from it. This will help you understand that your energy is not something to be given away freely. Rather, it is something to be tended, nourished, and honored.

—

CHAPTER 15

PROTECTING YOUR ENERGY & STAYING RESOURCED

Your energy is one of your most valuable resources, yet it is often the first thing sacrificed. Energy reserves are either spent or replenished with every interaction, task, conversation, or environment. When you move through life without awareness of this, you may find yourself giving from an empty cup. You wind up exhausted, overwhelmed, and unable to show up and be present for the parts of life that matter most.

Protecting your energy does not mean isolating yourself or avoiding all draining people and situations. It means becoming intentional about where your energy goes, how you spend it, and who you allow close to it. Instead of allowing yourself to be pulled in every direction or offering your emotional bandwidth to anyone who demands it, you choose where, how, and with whom you are giving time, attention, and grounded presence to. Then you can remain in an aligned and replenished state of being. This is an act of deep self-respect.

When your energy withdrawals exceed your energy deposits, the nervous system shifts into survival mode. Everything feels harder and even simple daily tasks can feel overwhelming. If you stay in that state long enough, mornings can begin with dread: waking already tired, bracing yourself for the day ahead.

I remember a time in my life when my body was completely exhausted, weary to the bone, but my nervous system was stuck in survival mode, and therefore unable to access deep, rejuvenating rest. The guilt and shame that followed only deepened the depletion. I wondered why even small things felt so difficult and draining. Operating in survival mode from that level of exhaustion meant that feeling grounded and centered was far out of reach. Presence and gratitude, which we discuss in the next chapter, felt nearly impossible.

Learning to protect your energy is not optional. It is essential for well-being, nervous system regulation, and long-term resilience. Boundaries become a central tool here. You learn what your daily capacity is, and as your nervous system heals, your capacity will naturally shift. Some days you will be able to hold more and some days less. Just honor that flow. Eventually you will feel able to handle more stress, more energy expenditure, and more risk. What is important here is to trust and honor your capacity in the moment. Only say yes when it works with your energy budget.

Replenish your energy before it is completely drained by taking small moments throughout the day, ensuring that your energy bank stays supported. Rest, nourishment, and moments of joy all support restoring energy, as well as micro-moments such as deep breaths, pauses, movement, or stillness. If you wait until you crash, recovery will always take longer.

Take notice of the early signs of depletion: irritability, fogginess, difficulty concentrating, feeling ungrounded, and losing your footing in the present moment. These are cues to pause and care for yourself, not signals to push through. Ultimately your life will feel more productive and fulfilling when you are experiencing daily life with energy in the bank. Pushing through complete burnout will only get you so far, and eventually your body and your nervous system will say, *enough is enough*.

Understanding Energy Drains

To protect your energy, you must first identify what drains it, but you do not need to identify every energy drain right now. Simply noticing one is enough. Here are some common drains that you may experience. You may recognize some of these immediately, and others may not apply. That is okay. Learning what to be aware of is a key part of protecting your energy.

People Who Take without Giving in Return (Emotional Dumping)
This can look like someone unloading their problems onto you without awareness or reciprocity, giving you the chance to speak about your own life. They feel better afterward but you feel completely drained.

Work That Conflicts with Your Values
Unrealistic workloads, constant new tasks, feeling like there are not enough hours in the day, or jobs that do not align with your integrity or purpose can drain a tremendous amount of energy and feel demoralizing.

Overexposure to News or Social Media
Internalizing feelings of anger, sadness, or dread. Getting dragged into negativity, outrage cycles, or online conflict in unproductive and often unkind conversations, sometimes with people we have never even met. People online might bully, talk rudely and sarcastically, and act self-righteously. Interacting with that sends the nervous system into survival mode and drains emotional bandwidth. Ask yourself, *Would I say this to a friend?*

Lack of Sleep

Sleep is foundational, being one of the most critical pieces in the overall puzzle of human health and happiness. Chronic deprivation leads to chronic stress, burnout, and a dysregulated nervous system. It erodes emotional resilience, cognitive clarity, and perhaps even the ability to find joy in life. It is impossible to stay resourced without meaningful rest.

Poor Nourishment

Rushed meals, processed food, skipped meals, or eating on the go all leave our bodies feeling depleted and can weaken nervous system steadiness.

Cluttered or Chaotic Environments

Research consistently links clutter with increased stress as it can feel hard to relax. Your environment affects your nervous system regulation more than you may realize.

Putting Everyone Else's Needs before Your Own

This can happen easily when parenting or caretaking, if you are stuck in people-pleasing or martyr roles, or you have trouble setting boundaries. Giving from an empty cup creates resentment, burnout, and emotional exhaustion.

Becoming aware of these drains allows you to limit or avoid them and make choices that keep your energy intact. Giving from an empty cup is not sustainable, and remember, you are worthy of a full cup. If any of these patterns feel familiar, let that recognition land gently. Awareness does not require immediate change.

Practices to Stay Resourced

Start your day with a deposit. Pick one small nourishing ritual before you give energy to anyone else. Enjoy a quiet cup of coffee or tea. Write in a journal. Offer gratitude. Take a short leisurely walk in nature, or do a breathing exercise or short meditation.

Check in with yourself throughout the day. What energized you? What drained you? Adjust accordingly going forward.

Schedule rest before you need rest. Make a regular practice of blocking out time for rest and recovery. This can look like a few minutes in between tasks or occasionally setting aside a whole day. Short moments of recovery prevent burnout and keep your nervous system unclenched.

Hold boundaries in draining conversations. Limit your time, protect your emotional space by making sure that you are not internalizing their emotions and drama, and respond from regulation rather than reacting from overload.

Mix in nourishing meals that support your body on a deeper level. Give yourself time to sit down and enjoy the food you are eating.

Notice what nourishes versus depletes. Be honest with yourself about the environments, people, and inputs such as news and social media that your nervous system thrives in and the ones that it doesn't.

You are not selfish for guarding your energy. You are worthy of it, and ultimately your loved ones will benefit much more if you give from a state of overflow rather than depletion. You become a steady presence, rooting into another deep form of self-respect.

Energy Vampires

Energy vampires are people who consistently drain your mental, emotional, or physical energy, often without intending to or having any awareness that they are doing so. They may be highly negative, chronically needy, manipulative, dramatic, inconsistent, or complain excessively. Your body often notices before your mind: subtle tightening, shallow breathing, or dread before seeing them. If you are noticing tension or resistance as you read this, pause for a breath. Your nervous system may be recognizing a familiar pattern.

Take note of how you feel after you have an interaction with someone. Do you feel lighter or heavier? Do you feel energized or depleted? Does your general outlook feel more positive or negative? Do you feel anxious or at peace?

How to Navigate Energy Vampires

- Set boundaries around time and topics. This can sound like, "I have about fifteen minutes for you then I really need to head out," or "I don't have the bandwidth to talk about that right now."

- Ground before and after the interaction, using deep breaths to move the heavy energy through you.

- Remind yourself, "This is not mine."

- Visualize energetic protection around yourself.

Emotional Dumping as an Energy Drain

As we discussed in a previous chapter, emotional dumping occurs when someone unloads their raw, heavy emotions onto you without consent or awareness of your capacity to receive it. It is a one-sided release that catches you off guard and leaves you overwhelmed while giving them temporary relief.

When faced with emotional dumping:

- Check your capacity first.

- Interrupt gently if needed, stating that you just do not have the space or energy right now.

- If that feels too direct, then try to redirect the conversation or excuse yourself.

- Avoid predictable dumping scenarios, at the very least in times when you are depleted and do not have the capacity to protect yourself.

Recognizing Emotional Manipulation

Emotional manipulation includes subtle or overt behaviors that distort truth or evoke guilt, confusion, or self-doubt. These patterns often originate from another person's own wounds or dysregulation, not from your shortcomings. Being able to recognize the behaviors for what they are will bring a new level of awareness to situations so you will be better able to protect yourself.

Common forms of emotional manipulation include:

- Blame shifting: The other person twists a situation around to point the blame for a situation at someone else.

- Gaslighting: One person undermines another person's perception of reality. This can make you question your own mind and even your memories of past situations.

- Deflecting: The subject is changed to avoid the subject at hand.

- Minimizing: Your feelings are dismissed or downplayed.

- Projecting: Someone's behavior or feelings are passed on to another person.

- Self-victimizing: The other person turns themselves into the victim so that you feel guilty.

Awareness allows you to stay centered and prevents you from absorbing dynamics that weaken your energy and override your intuition. Recognizing these patterns is not about labeling or blaming; it is about protecting your nervous system from carrying what was never yours to hold.

You are worthy of a life where your energy is protected, nourished, and honored. When you guard your energy, you are supporting your nervous system and your overall well-being. You become a steady presence, giving from overflow rather than depletion and rooting deeper into self-respect.

Nervous System Reset: Cord Cutting

Cord cutting is a symbolic practice used to release unhealthy energetic attachments to people, situations, or past experiences. These energetic cords can be imagined as emotional or energetic ties that keep you connected to something that no longer serves your well-being. When left unaddressed, these attachments drain your energy, keep your nervous system stuck in old patterns, and make it harder to move forward.

By symbolically cutting these cords through intentional visualization or ritual, you signal to your mind and body that you are reclaiming your energy and moving on from that which no longer serves you. This practice supports nervous system regulation because it helps the body let go of lingering stress responses connected to unresolved traumas, unhealthy relationships, and old patterns or habits.

Remember, these practices are an invitation, not a requirement. If at any point it feels like too much, give yourself permission to pause.

You can keep this practice simple, taking a few minutes for quick visualization. Or turn it into a more ceremonial experience, creating a meaningful ritual with intentional space and presence. You do not need to visualize perfectly; your intention is enough.

The Practice

1. Create a calming environment. Sit in a comfortable place. If you would like, brew a favorite tea, light a candle, use a smudge, or anything that helps you feel grounded.

2. Close your eyes and take a few slow breaths. Let your body settle. Allow your thoughts to soften.

3. Visualize the cords. Imagine the energetic cords attached to your body, each one representing a person, situation, memory, or pattern that drains you. See them clearly, pulsing with energy.

4. Cut or release the cords with compassion. Visualize yourself gently detaching each cord, one by one, releasing from a place of clarity and compassion, not anger.

5. As you continue to do your breathwork, release the cords on each exhale while mentally naming what you are releasing: *I release the need for approval. I release this old pattern. I release this draining connection.*

6. Reclaim your energy. After releasing the final cord, place your hands over your heart or center and affirm: *I reclaim my energy.*

7. Take a few grounding breaths and open your eyes when you are ready. Notice how your body feels afterward. Do you feel lighter, clearer, or more spacious?

You can also do a shorter version of this practice in the shower, visualizing the cords dissolving or washing away with the water.

Journal Prompts

Notice

- Do you notice early signs that your energy is beginning to run low? What does depletion feel like in your body? What do you typically do when that feeling arises? When you feel depleted, what do you usually do: push through, withdraw, ask for support, or something else?

- Who or what leaves you feeling drained after an interaction? Who or what leaves you feeling nourished?

- What makes you feel supported, replenished, or restored?

Reflect

- Where in your life are you giving from an empty cup?

- What emotions or situations do you tend to absorb from others that are not actually yours to hold?

Integrate

- What is one energy drain you can gently begin reducing this week? What small shift would make the biggest impact?

- What would protecting your energy look like if it were an act of self-respect rather than self-defense?

- What is one small act of restoration you could commit to this week?

Rewiring Your Outlook

My energy is sacred.

Going Forward

Each time you notice a drain, honor your capacity, or step away from an interaction that overwhelms your system, you are teaching your body that your well-being matters. Over time, your inner world becomes more stable, less reactive, and far more resourced. You live from overflow rather than depletion, making decisions from clarity instead of survival. This is how your nervous system learns that safety is not something you occasionally experience, but rather something you actively create.

As you move forward, remember that you are worthy of a life that does not leave you feeling depleted. Every boundary you set, every moment of rest you choose, and every unhealthy attachment you release is a step toward reclaiming your energy and your sense of self. The more you honor the truth of your needs, the more grounded, steady, and empowered you become.

Now that you've learned how to preserve and replenish your energy, you are ready to explore the next layer of nervous system wealth: presence and gratitude. When your energy is protected and your nervous system is resourced, you gain the capacity to notice the joys of life that were once buried under exhaustion. Presence becomes possible. Gratitude becomes accessible. The next chapter will guide you into these practices, creating a sense of inner abundance that grows from the inside out.

—

CHAPTER 16

HAPPINESS, PRESENCE, GRATITUDE & NERVOUS SYSTEM WEALTH

When we understand that happiness is not a destination we arrive at someday, nor a reward given after completing certain milestones, something inside us softens and we can breathe a little easier. Happiness is not something we must earn or be granted by others. It is a state of being that we must give ourselves permission to be in.

We learned how to take an active role in our other emotions, and we can apply that to happiness as well. However, if there are still wounds around worthiness, belonging, or self-respect, allowing ourselves to feel genuinely happy may be a struggle.

Sometimes we notice ourselves in a low mood without a clear cause. In those moments, it's often not the present day that's heavy, but residue from years spent in survival mode, when being on edge was the baseline. Awareness creates the opening. Choice creates the shift. When we recognize the pattern, we can move from *I have to* into *I get to*, and the nervous system begins to soften.

Happiness is deeply tied to perspective, presence, and the state of your nervous system, as the body must feel safe to experience joy. Being in a state of happiness is not forcing positivity or ignoring real pain. You are shifting your perspective, the lens through which you see the world, while weaving in gratitude and presence. This is softening the nervous system enough to feel safe and allow in moments of joy.

When you rely on outside sources for happiness through things like external achievements, approval, or instant gratification, then you must chase it, and it often becomes fleeting. When happiness arises from the inside, it becomes stable, rooted, and sustainable. It becomes something you carry rather than something you chase. You are more even keeled going through life, even in times of difficulty or uncertainty.

From this space, joy reveals itself in the simplest moments: warm sunlight on your face, the comfort of tea in your hands, a soft blanket, watching your kids play, or noticing beautiful flowers on a table. Even setbacks can be seen through a different lens, not as failures, but pauses or redirections designed to serve our highest good.

Contentment as the Bridge to Presence, Gratitude & Joy

Many people think joy arrives in a single breakthrough moment, a sudden shift, or a dramatic awakening, but for a nervous system that has lived in survival mode, joy is far too large a leap. When the body has spent years bracing for impact, staying hypervigilant or chronically overwhelmed, joy can feel unsafe, unfamiliar, or unrealistic.

This is why many people struggle with happiness even when life starts to "get better." The body does not automatically trust the new ease as it is still waiting for something to go wrong. This is where contentment becomes the quiet and steady essential middle ground. It is the overlooked state that bridges survival mode with genuine joy. It is gentle enough for a dysregulated system to access, yet powerful enough to slowly reshape your inner reality.

From Dysregulation to Contentment

Dysregulation keeps you stuck in the past or future, replaying old wounds or anticipating new threats. In this state, stillness feels uncomfortable, joy feels out of reach, happiness feels unsafe, gratitude feels forced, and presence feels impossible. When the body is dysregulated, it is not trying to feel good, it is just trying to survive.

Initially, finding contentment is going to feel more accessible to your nervous system. It is the feeling that nothing is wrong right now. Feeling content is small, soft, and approachable. Your nervous system is no longer bracing, perhaps your shoulders and jaw relax, and your body realizes, *I'm okay in this moment*. There is an absence of pressure and urgency, and everything right now is enough. Contentment is the quiet calm that allows the body to experience ease without demanding expansion, rebuilding your capacity to feel.

Happiness can trigger thoughts of unworthiness that sound like, *I don't deserve this yet* or, *If I feel good, something bad will happen*. Being in a state of contentment invites your body to pause and rest here in this moment, showing your body a micro-moment of safety.

Contentment is not complacency. You are not giving up or settling for less. Rather, you are establishing the emotional foundation upon which your desires can grow without fear. You expand sustainably from safety, not survival mode, and that begins with contentment.

Contentment lives in small, ordinary moments:

- The first warm sip of morning tea
- A soft blanket around your shoulders
- Your child laughing in the next room
- Sunlight on your skin
- A clean kitchen at night
- Hearing a favorite song
- A fresh breeze through an open window

These micro-moments teach your nervous system safety, and the more often you experience them, the more your body trusts peace. Feeling content teaches your system that you are safe, you are enough, and that you are allowed to feel okay.

Mindfulness as the Path to Presence

Where contentment is a state of ease, mindfulness is the practice that helps you access that ease more deliberately. Mindfulness is gentle attention, noticing rather than judging. Over time, mindfulness strengthens the nervous system's sense of safety, softening the reflex to predict danger and allowing your body to trust the present moment.

Presence is a state of being fully engaged in the moment. Mindfulness is the path that leads you there, building a bridge between your nervous system and the present. It strengthens your ability to return to yourself when your mind drifts into worry or memory. Mindfulness is the simple, compassionate act of returning your awareness to what is happening right now: your breath, your senses, your thoughts, and your surroundings, without trying to change any of it. Mindfulness turns contentment into a practice and presence into a pattern.

Rooting into Presence

Once the body trusts that the moment is safe, presence becomes available, as your nervous system is no longer overwhelmed. Of course, presence is not always easy. The mind can quickly drift into fear of the future or old memories that bring shame or sadness. But presence is a choice, one that becomes more accessible with practice. When we root into presence, everyday moments become extraordinary: a child's laughter, birdsong outside the window, autumn leaves, a shared meal, a conversation with someone we love. In presence, we remember that we cannot change the past, though we can change how we hold it, and that the future has yet to be written.

Presence begins with noticing:

- Feel the warmth of your hands around a mug.
- Hear the sound of a storm outside.
- Feel the joy of laughter and the connection of a hug.
- Really see a beautiful view.

If presence feels difficult, pause for a moment. Reconnect with your senses: What can you see, touch, hear, smell, and taste? This anchors you back into your body and out of the spiraling thoughts of the mind.

Presence as a Foundation for Gratitude

Gratitude deepens presence, and presence strengthens gratitude; they feed each other. Presence anchors us into the fullness of each moment; gratitude enriches the moment we are in. Both are directly connected to the nervous system. When we are regulated, our senses sharpen, our awareness expands, and we are not trapped in loops of past or future thinking. We can truly experience life as it is unfolding. Gratitude is simply the recognition of something good in the present moment, but accessing grateful awareness can feel difficult if your body is stuck in fear. Contentment, mindfulness, and presence all give your system the stability required to root into moments of gratitude.

Gratitude is a powerful interrupter of stress cycles. One grateful thought can shift the entire trajectory of your day. Negativity compounds, but so does gratitude. Even something like a sink full of dishes can be approached with irritation or with appreciation. You can shift your perspective to something like *these dishes represent food, family, and abundance*. You are choosing to experience the moment from a place of presence and gratitude, and that makes all the difference in your overall outlook and mindset. The moment your perspective shifts, your body shifts with it. Your shoulders drop, your breath deepens, and tension softens. These small shifts give your nervous system safety cues, restoring resilience and increasing your capacity for whatever comes next.

Gratitude is not forced positivity or the denial of difficult situations. It is the acknowledgment that amidst struggle, there are still things to appreciate. It brings awareness to all the things in your life that are good despite the difficulties. It interrupts the spiral of stress and gently shifts your perspective.

In moments of deep hardship, it can feel hard to find things that we are grateful for. We get caught up in resentment and despair over the current circumstances, wishing that things could be different. But if we dig deep into these moments, we can always find something good to acknowledge. Even in pain, we can be grateful for breath, for water, for sunlight, and for the strength that carried us this far. Gratitude softens our experience in this world. It also softens our relationship with ourselves, becoming a core part of healing self-worth and building nervous system wealth.

Gratitude increases nervous system safety, allowing more contentment, more presence, and more joy. From this place, anxiety about the future naturally softens. And when you can live here more often, rooted and regulated, you open the door to new possibilities and expansion.

Joy Emerges from Gratitude

Joy arises when gratitude softens the body enough to feel expansive.

It is built from:

- Nervous system safety
- Emotional openness
- Steady presence
- A sense of sufficiency
- Inner quiet
- Alignment with the moment

Joy is not the first step. It is the result of contentment and presence being repeated, practiced, and embodied. When gratitude becomes habitual, your internal landscape becomes kinder, steadier, and more aware, then joy has room to grow.

Joy is expansive, blooming from safety, presence, and repeated moments of rooting into self-worth. In this way, joy becomes the culmination of contentment practiced, presence chosen, gratitude embodied. Nervous system wealth is built on this internal abundance, where you can access peace, presence, and joy regardless of external circumstance.

Dysregulation → **Contentment** → **Mindfulness** → **Presence** → **Gratitude** → **Joy**

Finding Comfort in Silence

Silence can be uncomfortable for many people. You may know someone who fills every pause with words, always has a TV or radio on, or turns immediately to their phone whenever quiet arises. This is not a flaw; it is a nervous system coping strategy. Quiet brings them face-to-face with their thoughts and emotions, and so the constant noise gives them a distraction from that. If they can keep the distractions, noise, and conversations going, then they do not have to listen to their inner voice. But silence is where clarity grows. It is also where the nervous system learns to rest.

To move past the discomfort of quiet, you must decide that you finally want to listen. Start small and begin gently. Sit outside for a few minutes. Tune in to your senses, noticing what you hear and feel. Then, slowly bear witness to your thoughts without judgment. Let the silence hold you, building safety slowly. Compassion and patience are essential as you teach your nervous system that silence is safe, a place of clarity and peace. Over time, your body will learn that quiet is not a threat but a refuge.

Nervous System Reset: Water Gratitude Ritual

There is a long-held belief across many cultures that our words, intentions, and blessings can influence the energy of water, and even its structure. Dr. Masaru Emoto explored this idea in *The Secret Life of Water*, where he photographed frozen water crystals after exposing them to different words, prayers, and music. Water that received loving words, such as "love," "thank you," or "gratitude," formed beautifully symmetrical crystals. Water exposed to harsh messages, such as "hate" or "anger," formed distorted, fragmented shapes.

While his work has been debated, the underlying idea remains powerful when we consider that the human body is made mostly of water. If intention affects water externally, imagine the impact that kind words and grateful thoughts may have internally.

The Practice

This gratitude ritual is simple, quick, and deeply regulating. You can weave it into your daily routine before a meal, with your morning tea, or anytime you want to shift into presence.

1. Hold your cup or plate gently, placing your hands around it (being mindful of temperature).

2. Slow your breath. Allow your body to soften.

3. Visualize warmth and positive energy flowing from your hands into the water, tea, or food in front of you.

4. Offer a word or blessing of gratitude, such as:

> *Thank you for this nourishment.*
>
> *I am grateful for this meal.*
>
> *Thank you for refreshing and sustaining me.*
>
> *Thank you for supporting my body with what it needs.*

5. Savor the experience. As you drink or eat, notice the taste, the temperature, the way your body feels receiving nourishment.

This small practice encourages you to slow down and be in presence, taking the time to really appreciate the nourishment in front of you. It slows down the nervous system and infuses a moment of everyday life with intention. Gratitude softens your internal state, and this ritual helps you anchor that gratitude directly into your body.

Journal Prompts

Notice

- What does contentment feel like in your nervous system? When was the last time you felt this sensation?

- What sensory experiences anchor you in the moment most easily: touch, sound, smell, sight, or taste?

- When you slow down and become present, what emotions arise? Do any of those emotions feel unfamiliar or unsafe?

Reflect

- What thoughts, worries, or patterns tend to pull you out of the present moment? Are there specific moments in life where staying present feels difficult?

- Think of something you genuinely appreciate, such as a warm shower, a beautiful flower, a peaceful moment, or a great cup of coffee. When you focus on that appreciation, what shifts in your body?

- Are there areas of your life where you've been telling yourself you must wait to feel happy? What conditions have you placed around your own joy?

Integrate

- Where in your life do you feel the greatest ease? How can you cultivate more of that feeling?

- What would it feel like to let happiness be a state you practice rather than a reward you earn?

Rewiring Your Outlook

I am grateful for this moment.

Going Forward

As you move forward from this chapter, remember that presence, contentment, and gratitude are not destinations you must reach. They are states of being.

Each moment of contentment and presence is a softening of your nervous system. Each moment of gratitude is a shift in the lens through which you experience your life. These practices gather strength over time, shaping your inner landscape, building your resilience, and creating space for joy to flourish naturally rather than being forced.

You now have the tools to anchor your body in safety and your mind in self-worth. This foundation is what makes expansion possible. With contentment as your steady ground and presence as your compass, you no longer have to wait for happiness to arrive. You can cultivate it from within. Let these practices carry you into the next part of your journey, where you begin to design outward from the inner work you've done here.

Before moving into this next layer of growth, take a moment to notice what arises in you. Expansion can feel exciting, but it can also feel vulnerable. If you sense hesitation, it may simply mean your system is asking for more integration. There is no fixed timeline here. You can return to earlier chapters at any time, deepening what feels unfinished. Growth is not linear, and revisiting foundational work is not a step backward. When you sense that you can remain connected to yourself as you stretch, these next steps may feel less like a leap and more like a natural unfolding.

Now we turn toward a new layer of nervous system wealth: being seen. Rooted visibility and authentic expression ask you to step into your life with a deeper level of truth and courage, not from urgency or performance, but from regulation, worthiness, and alignment. As your inner world becomes steadier, your voice strengthens. Your expression becomes clearer. The life you desire begins to feel not only possible, but inevitable.

In the next chapter, I invite you into this expansion: how to express yourself without abandoning yourself; how to be visible without collapsing into old wounds; and how to design a life that reflects the truth of who you are. You've built the inner foundation. Now we begin building the life that grows from it and aligns with your true self.

DESIGN

—

*Creating Your Life from
Embodied Worthiness*

—

CHAPTER 17

ROOTED VISIBILITY, AUTHENTIC EXPRESSION & SOUL-ALIGNED SUCCESS

When your nervous system is dysregulated, visibility can feel dangerous. Being seen feels like exposure, and so it seems like the safest option is staying small and unnoticeable.

When your nervous system is regulated, visibility is not a threat. You are rooted in safety, and so sharing your voice no longer feels dangerous.

Authentic expression arises when you are sharing from a place of deep alignment, speaking from your true self. You are not shifting your message to seek approval or avoid judgment. When you share from this aligned place, you are not bracing for judgment and your nervous system understands, *I am safe to be myself here*.

There will always be people who disagree with you, especially in the age of social media, where anonymity emboldens cruelty. But when you are experiencing this visibility through deeply aligned authentic expression and rooted in self-worth, then negative comments no longer bother you. As you continue integrating the inner work from earlier chapters, your voice begins to shift. It becomes less an extension of old wounds and more an expression of your emerging wholeness. Self-worth and self-respect deepen gradually, in ways that feel steady and grounded.

If visibility feels frightening, there is a good chance you experienced wounds tied to shame, criticism, humiliation, ridicule, or rejection. We are afraid to be seen because we do not want to feel these wounds again. We think: *What if someone makes fun of me*? It feels safer to remain unseen in the shadows, but is that how we want to continue to go through life? We all have gifts to contribute to the world, but we cannot share them unless we become willing to put ourselves out there.

Every chapter you have completed so far has prepared you for this one. All the self-exploration, nervous system regulation work, self-worth healing, and energy protection have created the internal conditions necessary for visibility to finally feel possible.

Visibility wounds are nervous system wounds and therefore require nervous system healing techniques. When your nervous system feels safe, self-expression flows. You are no longer silencing your voice. You can express yourself without worrying, and you can do it without editing to receive approval or avoid negative comments and potential conflict. If you experience rejection, you do not dwell on it or collapse into it. You return to center and move forward unshaken, reminding yourself that not everyone is going to be your match.

The Visibility Window & the Cost of Self-Editing

Just as the nervous system has a range where it can stay regulated, visibility also has a threshold. Within this range, expression feels safe. Outside it, the body moves into protection. This is your visibility window. When you are within your visibility window, you can share honestly, speak clearly, advocate for yourself, and express your ideas without slipping into a sympathetic nervous system state.

But when you are pushed outside that window through judgment, scrutiny, conflict, performance pressure, or even your own inner critic, then your nervous system reacts as if visibility is dangerous. This often comes from old wounds, where being seen meant that you were shamed, ridiculed, ignored, punished, or misunderstood.

When you move outside your visibility window, the body enters a survival response. You may feel one or several changes, including:

- Throat tightening
- Stomach dropping
- A rush of heat
- A spike of self-doubt
- Mental fog or blanking
- The urge to shrink, hide, or disappear
- The impulse to talk too much, too fast
- Trouble forming sentences
- Feeling suddenly "not yourself"

These are not character flaws; they are nervous system adaptations. Your body is simply trying to protect you in the ways it knows best from the dangers visibility once held. Instead of interpreting this response as *something is wrong with me*, begin recognizing it as *my nervous system thinks being seen is unsafe*. This awareness opens the door to healing.

Self-Editing: The Nervous System's Visibility Armor

When your visibility window is small, you naturally develop strategies to stay feeling safe. Self-editing is one of the most common.

Self-editing is:

- Overthinking every sentence
- Toning down your truth
- Reshaping your voice to avoid conflict
- Diluting your opinions
- Cutting out emotion
- Apologizing for everything
- Staying vague so no one can disagree
- Trying to sound "acceptable," "nice," or "easy"
- Talking yourself out of sharing at all

Self-editing often begins early when childhood visibility was met with criticism, shame, humiliation, mockery, punishment, or rejection. The nervous system learns that being yourself is dangerous and you must reduce yourself to feel safe. Self-editing is not a personality trait; it is a survival response. And while it once protected you, it slowly becomes a cage.

How Visibility Wounds Shape Adult Expression

When a child's authenticity was punished, ignored, dismissed, or minimized, adulthood brings patterns like keeping ideas to yourself, struggling to post online, replaying conversations afterward, being overly agreeable, overexplaining, or assuming everyone is judging you. These are nervous system scars, not failures. But visibility wounds do not disappear with age; they shift with healing.

Widening the Visibility Window

Healing your relationship with visibility begins by gently widening your visibility window. You do not expand visibility tolerance through force. You expand it through gentle, repeated safety cues. This can look like speaking one sentence of truth or adding your opinion to a conversation. Perhaps you send the message instead of rewriting it three times, or you share something small online. Voicing your preference in low-stakes moments and noticing when you want to shrink, then choosing to stay, are more ways to widen your visibility window.

Each time you express yourself from a regulated place, your visibility window widens. Your system learns that being seen can be safe. This is a slow and lasting rewiring of your nervous system.

Self-Editing versus Authentic Expression

Self-editing is what happens when your visibility window is small. It fractures the connection that you have with your inner truth, forcing you to abandon what you know, feel, or believe to be accepted. But as your visibility window expands, trust in yourself can grow, and when you remain within that window, then authentic expression can emerge.

Authentic expression is not about oversharing or impulsive honesty. It is when your inner truth and your outer words match. Authentic expression reinforces that connection, rooting you into your worth, your voice, and your nervous system's sense of safety. When your visibility window expands, self-editing softens naturally. Your voice becomes clearer, your presence feels steadier, and your expression becomes aligned instead of filtered through fear. When visibility no longer overwhelms you, soul-aligned success becomes possible.

Advocating for Yourself

Advocating for yourself can feel uncomfortable at first, maybe even selfish, especially if you come from patterns of people-pleasing, fawning, or minimizing your needs. But self-advocacy is simply another expression of self-worth. You are honoring your needs and telling your body that your needs matter too.

Self-advocacy reinforces your boundaries, builds self-trust and self-confidence, and teaches your nervous system that speaking up does not equal danger. It doesn't have to start with big, charged conversations. Often, it begins in small, low-stakes moments, asking again when your water is forgotten at a restaurant, requesting clarity from a doctor, sharing which movie you actually want to see, or saying *no* to something that doesn't feel right. Even asking for help without apologizing can be an act of nervous system repair.

The more that you advocate for yourself, the more comfortable you will be doing it. Each time you advocate for yourself in these gentle ways, your body learns that your needs are not a burden. You are worthy of having your needs seen and heard, and you always were.

The Energetic Cost of Self-Silencing

Self-silencing is one of the most subtle yet exhausting forms of self-abandonment. Every time you swallow your truth, dilute your words, soften your edges, or pretend to agree to avoid discomfort, your body carries the weight of that suppression. What looks like peacekeeping on the outside often feels like internal tension, resentment, or depletion on the inside.

When you silence yourself, your nervous system registers it as a threat. The body tightens. The breath shortens. Your mind begins replaying the moment, thinking about what you should have said, or what you wished you had expressed. Instead of release and clarity, there is holding and rumination. The energy that should move through your voice becomes trapped, which over time becomes an energetic expense.

You may feel:
- Chronically tired for no clear reason
- Overstimulated in social situations
- Resentful toward people who "don't listen"
- Disconnected from your desires
- Muted, dimmed, or invisible
- Anxious before conversations
- Unable to rest even in a calm environment

This is because your body is expending enormous amounts of energy to maintain an internal performance that does not match your truth. Self-silencing narrows your visibility window, shrinks your sense of self, and teaches your nervous system to expect suppression instead of expression.

How to Start Small with Visibility

Widening your visibility window requires micro-expressions of truth rather than giant leaps. This teaches your body that being seen can feel grounded, not dangerous.

Like advocating for yourself, you start with low-stakes moments: Share one sentence of truth. Post an authentic caption that was not crafted for approval. Or allow your presence to take up more space. Say something that you have been avoiding or might not normally say, such as "that does not work for me" or "actually, I would prefer something else." Ask for something that you need: a moment of time, support, clarification, or maybe just a refill on your water.

These tiny acts might seem insignificant, but every micro-moment widens your visibility window, strengthens your self-trust, and slowly rewires the old belief that being seen is unsafe. Healing happens in increments, not leaps, one small moment at a time.

The Somatic Signature of Authenticity

Your body knows the difference between truth and performance long before your mind does. When you are speaking or expressing from authenticity, your body feels:

- Grounded through the feet
- Open through the chest
- Steady in your breath
- Warm in the heart space
- Clear in the throat
- Connected to your words rather than detached from them
- Present, not performing
- Spacious, not constricted

Authentic expression has a sense of alignment between your inner truth and your outer voice. You may feel both vulnerable and empowered but not threatened, and your message feels rooted in your body.

When you are performing, self-editing, or expressing from fear, the body reacts differently. You may experience some of the following:

- Shallow breath
- Tightening in the throat
- Clenching in the jaw
- Collapsing shoulders

- Fidgeting or shrinking
- Racing thoughts
- A sense of watching yourself instead of being yourself

The more you practice rooted visibility, the more familiar the somatic signature of authenticity becomes. Over time, your body begins to prefer this state: the clarity and ease, as well as feeling grounded. Authenticity becomes safe and nourishing.

Soul-Aligned Success: A Worthy Redesign

You may feel that your life up until now has been a chain of events you simply reacted to, living on autopilot, adapting to circumstances, and surviving more than choosing. When you operate from a wounded nervous system, the choices that you make stem from old traumas, patterns, habits, and coping mechanisms. This might lead you to choose jobs, stay in relationships, and fill your schedule with obligations that do not align. They are decisions based on fear and what is familiar to your nervous system.

But now you are ready to intentionally create from a state of inherent worthiness. You are no longer creating from survival mode. You are shifting from the victim of circumstance to the intentional designer. Soul-aligned success is not built from urgency, fear, or comparison. It emerges when your nervous system feels safe enough to expand and your self-worth is strong enough to choose alignment over expectation.

When you were operating from a wounded nervous system, your choices were shaped by old traumas, coping mechanisms, patterns of self-abandonment, scarcity, and familiarity rather than desire. A dysregulated body chooses what feels safe, not what feels aligned.

When you return to regulation, the possibilities of your life open. Your desires become accessible and creativity becomes possible, as you are no longer shackled to limiting beliefs. You choose work, relationships, environments, and habits that nourish you instead of drain you. Over time, this becomes self-sustaining, as our choices will better support our well-being and self-worth, and then we experience deeper nervous system healing and can expand our horizons even further. This is nervous system wealth.

You make aligned choices → You feel safe → Your capacity grows → You make more aligned choices

Nervous System Reset: Values Inventory

The purpose of this practice is to help you gain clarity around your core values. Many of our values were inherited, conditioned, or created out of survival rather than choice. But now we can ask whether those values still align with who we are and who we are becoming. When we take time to name our values with intention, we can embody them in our daily lives, and when our values match our actions, the body feels that coherence. Integrity is what your nervous system feels when your actions match your values. This felt sense of integrity brings calm, clarity, and grounded self-trust to the nervous system.

Values versus What You Value: A Helpful Distinction

Before you begin your values inventory, it can help to understand the difference between your core values and what you value in your daily life. While they sound similar, there is a slight difference, and they guide your nervous system and decisions in different ways.

Core values are deeper truths of who you are that tend to be stable and act as an internal compass. They are identity based and influence how you want to live. Examples of core values are honesty, compassion, peace, integrity, and freedom.

What you value, on the other hand, are the qualities, experiences, and environments that support your well-being. They are things that you care about, appreciate, or enjoy. This can look like cozy mornings, time to be creative, nature, beauty, a clean house, financial stability, comfort, adventure, meaningful conversations, and rest. What you value can shift over time, changing with the seasons, your environment, or different stages of life. These values are more flexible and situational, influencing how you spend your time from day to day.

When your core values and what you value are aligned, then your nervous system feels coherence and safety. When they are out of alignment, your body can register that as stress, tension and overwhelm. For example, you may value peace, but your life is chaotic. Or maybe you value connection, but you spend most of your time isolated.

Understanding both your core values and what you value can help you to design a life that honors both who you are and what nourishes you. When you can identify both layers, you can better design your daily habits, environment, goals, boundaries, life choices, and how you support your nervous system. You are aligning your core identity to your everyday reality.

Emotional Coherence

Emotional coherence is what happens when your inner world and your outer choices match. It is the state where your values, needs, and actions are aligned enough that your nervous system can relax into truth rather than brace against contradiction. When you live in a way that supports what matters most to you, your body experiences a sense of internal harmony: breath deepens, tension softens, and decisions feel clearer.

But when your actions contradict what you value, the body registers this mismatch as stress. You might say *yes* when your truth is *no*, stay silent when you value honesty, or keep peace externally while creating chaos inside. This lack of coherence is a nervous system message telling us where we are out of alignment.

Emotional coherence, then, becomes a compass. It helps you discern which choices nourish your self-worth and which ones pull you into self-abandonment. And this is where the difference between your core values and what you value in daily life becomes essential, because coherence is the space where the two meet.

The Practice

1. Find a quiet, comfortable place to sit. Bring a journal or piece of paper, and take a few grounding breaths to settle into your body.

2. Write down fifteen to twenty values that resonate with you. For example: freedom, honesty, connection, peace, generosity, respect.

3. Circle your top five. Sit with each one and notice what arises in your body.

4. Ask yourself:

   Do I feel currently aligned with this value?

   What daily actions support this value?

   When I imagine violating this value, what sensations do I feel? Tightness? Heat? Guilt? Anxiety?

   When I imagine living this value more fully, what shifts in my body?

5. Reflect on what no longer fits. Are there values on your list that no

longer resonate? Have you ever compromised on a value to stay safe, accepted, or invisible?

This practice helps you understand what your nervous system feels like when you are aligned, and what it feels like when you are not. When you honor what you truly value, you naturally feel more grounded, peaceful, and at home in your life.

Journal Prompts

Notice

- When you think about being visible, what happens in your body? Does visibility feel safe, or does it activate discomfort? If fear arises, what do you imagine might happen if you are fully seen?

- When you think about asking for what you need now, what emotions or body sensations arise? Does your voice want to shrink or expand?

- When your values and actions are aligned, how does your body respond?

Reflect

- When do you tend to self-edit the most? Around whom? What does your body fear will happen if you speak with your full voice?

- What has staying invisible protected you from in the past? What is it costing you now? How might your life expand if visibility no longer activated fear in your system?

- Can you recall a time when you stayed silent instead of speaking up? How did you feel when the moment passed you by? Now imagine yourself expressing your truth in that moment. How does your body feel in that version of the story?

Integrate

- When you imagine expressing your truth without self-editing, what becomes possible in your life?

- What is one low-stakes way you could practice visibility this week?

Rewiring Your Outlook

I express myself openly, grounded in my worth.

Going Forward

Stepping into rooted visibility is not about forcing yourself into the spotlight or suddenly becoming fearless. It is about returning to yourself slowly and gently, one honest moment at a time. As you strengthen the safety cues in your body, your capacity to be seen will naturally expand. What once felt threatening begins to feel possible, and eventually even liberating. Each moment of authentic expression becomes a micro-recalibration, teaching your nervous system that it is safe to speak, safe to take up space, safe to exist fully as yourself. From this grounded place, visibility becomes a natural extension of who you are when you no longer abandon your voice. And as you root deeper into your truth, the path ahead opens with a clarity and self-trust that was not accessible before.

When you reclaim your voice and honor your authentic expression, you step into a new phase of your healing where you no longer live by inherited expectations, survival patterns, or fear-based decisions. This is where creation becomes possible. The next chapter invites you to explore what your life looks like when it is designed from self-worth rather than self-protection, when your choices support your nervous system instead of overwhelming it, when your goals align with who you truly are, and when you choose expansion from a place of embodied self-worth rather than chasing achievement for external validation.

In this next chapter, we will explore how to design a life that reflects your values, honors your capacity, and supports the future you want to build. You will learn how to make decisions from a grounded place, how to align your ambitions with your inner compass, and how to create a path forward that feels nourishing, sustainable, and deeply yours. This is where your healing becomes your blueprint, and your self-worth becomes the foundation upon which your worthy life is built.

—

CHAPTER 18

CREATING A WORTHY LIFE

Creating is not reserved for artists, writers, or people who make things with their hands. You are creating every day, whether you realize it or not. You create through the choices you make, the boundaries you hold, the rhythms you keep, the way you speak to yourself, and the environments you shape around you. Your life itself is the canvas. You create through how you spend your time and energy, how you respond to challenges, how you care for your body, and how you relate to others.

From a nervous system perspective, creating is simply the act of shaping your experience from the inside out. When your body feels safe, supported, and worthy, the way you move through the world naturally begins to change. This chapter is not about producing something impressive; it's about consciously designing a life that feels aligned, sustainable, and true to you. You don't have to make something new to be a creator. You are creating simply by choosing how you live.

Creating From Grounded Worthiness

Most of us have spent years, perhaps even entire chapters of our lives, creating from urgency, fear, perfectionism, or the restless ache of feeling like we are not enough. In these states, it becomes an attempt to fix ourselves, earn worthiness, or outrun shame. We create to prove something, to avoid judgment, to gain approval, or to keep up with expectations that were never truly ours. But when your nervous system is regulated and you finally root into grounded worthiness, everything changes.

Creating from a sense of being enough means creating from wholeness. It allows your work, voice, and desires to become expressions of your inherent worth rather than attempts to compensate for imagined inadequacy. It is the shift from performing to expressing, from bracing to allowing, from pushing to creating. Grounded worthiness becomes the foundation upon which you can design and build a worthy life.

When you create from grounded worthiness, you recognize that your worth is inherent and unconditional. It is not something that must be earned through productivity or success. Recognizing this dramatically shifts the energetic tone of your creativity.

Creating from survival mode feels urgent, pressured, and exhausting. It often carries thoughts like:

> *I need this to be perfect.*
>
> *What will people think?*
>
> *I can't make a mistake.*
>
> *If this doesn't work, what does that say about me?*

Creating from grounded worthiness feels honest, spacious, inspired, and expressive, rather than forced, over-edited, and performative. You stop creating to earn your worthiness and start creating as an expression of it.

This frees you to take more creative risks as you are no longer held back by the fear of failure or worried about the reception of your ideas. You can follow inspiration, detach from outcomes, and trust your voice without bracing for impact. You don't need to be guaranteed success to begin, and you don't need to know how something will be received to share it.

Shifting into Grounded Worthiness Before You Create

Creating from grounded worthiness is less about doing something right and more about noticing the state you are creating from. Before you begin, it can be helpful to pause and sense what's driving the urge to act, whether it's fear, urgency, perfectionism, or simply a desire to be seen. A single grounding breath or moment of presence can remind your nervous system that you are safe here, and that your worth is not on the line. From that place, you can release attachment to outcomes, honor your energy as it is, and allow creation to unfold at a pace that feels sustainable.

Small steps and moments of acknowledgment along the way become acts of self-trust rather than pressure. This is how creation shifts from performance into presence.

Chasing Someone Else's Version of Success

Constantly trying to keep up with others connects your success to scarcity rather than abundance. You are living in a state of stress, constantly comparing and competing, needing external validation to prove your success. Staying in this cycle will make it almost impossible to honor your capacity as you will always be pushing to meet another person's version of success. You will feel like you are running a race without even knowing where the finish line is.

The constant exposure to social media can easily make us feel lack, jealousy, and greed by looking at the feeds of those seemingly more fortunate than us. We quickly forget that these moments shared on social media are often carefully curated, and you only see the good moments, not the messy ones.

Designing a Worthy Life

A worthy life is not curated for external validation. It is not shaped by pressure, comparison, or inherited expectations. It is not the life others say you should want. And when you stop comparing your nervous system's capacity to others, you can experience a soft expansion instead of pressure-based growth. You no longer feel the need to recover from your own life.

A worthy life is the outer expression of the inner healing you have done throughout this book. You are rooted in safety, self-worth, values-based decisions, meaningful connection, rest and play, emotional coherence, and aligned ambition.

When your nervous system has lived in survival mode, your life is often shaped by old traumas, coping mechanisms, familiar yet misaligned patterns, fear-based decisions, inherited beliefs, and external expectations. People stay in draining jobs or relationships because the nervous system clings to what is familiar, even when the familiar is painful.

But as your nervous system heals, a profound shift occurs. You become free to design a life that matches your values instead of your wounds. You stop choosing what keeps you small, avoids conflict, pleases others, and feels safest to your past self. Instead, you move toward what nourishes and expands you, aligns with your values, reflects your growth, and feels like the truth of who you are. This is a central part of nervous system wealth.

Reevaluating Your Reward System

We are shown through television, marketing, and social media that it is normal to use food, alcohol, and shopping as ways to celebrate, reward, or soothe. But many of these reward systems are dysregulation loops, giving us quick dopamine hits that we use to escape discomfort rather than nourish the self.

Our culture encourages this:

> *I deserve a drink after today.*
>
> *I earned this dessert.*
>
> *Retail therapy will fix this.*

These rewards soothe temporarily but erode long-term well-being, self-trust, and emotional stability. We end up chasing instant gratification again instead of reinforcing good habits, and eventually we may end up having unhealthy relationships with these things.

Aligned rewards, however, strengthen regulation. They might look like scheduling a massage, taking a long luxurious bath, buying fresh flowers, reading something that nourishes you, or choosing rest without "earning" it.

A worthy life includes worthy rewards. Ask yourself: Does this reward regulate me or dysregulate me? Does it replenish or deplete? Is this soothing or self-abandonment? Is this aligned with who I'm becoming?

Instant Gratification versus Long-Term Alignment

When our nervous system is on edge, we are more apt to look for instant gratification, wanting an immediate reward to offset our discomfort, getting a quick boost of dopamine in the process. Instant gratification is not a personal failure; it is a nervous system coping strategy. When your system feels unsafe, it seeks immediate relief through things like impulsive shopping, snacking even when you are not hungry, doomscrolling, or distraction.

You may get stuck in cycles of giving in, but afterward you feel like you have let yourself down. You then expect to disappoint yourself, leading to lower levels of self-trust. This keeps you in the loop of instant gratification even more as you seek temporary relief from discomfort.

Delayed gratification, on the other hand, is allowing yourself to make better choices that support your long-term success. It builds resilience, teaching your nervous system that discomfort is tolerable, safety is available, and that you can trust yourself to choose alignment over urgency. This isn't about deprivation; it's about choosing long-term alignment over short-term escape.

Foundations of a Worthy Life

A worthy life is not built through hustle, perfection, or constant self-improvement. It is built through regulation, alignment, and self-trust. It begins with a nervous system that feels safe enough to rest and respond rather than react. From there, meaning replaces pressure, and contribution becomes an expression of values rather than worth. Relationships are chosen for nourishment, honoring your boundaries and reflecting your worth. Rest and play are woven into daily rhythm, not postponed as rewards. Small, consistent behaviors reinforce identity more than grand resolutions. Values and boundaries become a compass, anchoring your life in integrity and inner truth. And beneath it all is the quiet courage to choose yourself again and again, not as an act of defiance, but as an act of embodied self-respect.

Nervous System Reset: Aligned Action Audit

This is a practice that you can use whenever you need to check in with yourself to determine whether a particular choice or action is aligned and supportive of your energy, values, and nervous system capacity. It teaches you to recognize the difference between acting from pressure in a reactive state and acting from alignment in grounded presence.

When your choices come from alignment, you feel rooted, centered, and connected. Your soul feels nourished. There is a natural sense of flow. When they come from urgency or self-pressure, you are choosing from survival mode, and your body often communicates constriction, tightness, or dread.

The Practice

The Aligned Action Audit brings you back to your internal compass so you can choose from truth instead of habit, fear, or external expectation.

1. Begin with a few grounding breaths. Let your shoulders drop. Feel your body connected to the ground beneath you. You are creating space for clarity to rise.

2. Bring the action or decision to mind. Observe it gently, not with urgency, but with curiosity.

3. Move through the following questions slowly, paying close attention to your body's immediate response before your mind begins to rationalize. Ask yourself:

- Does this action or decision feel expanding or constricting? Expansion often means alignment; constriction often signals pressure, fear, or overextension.

- Am I choosing this out of obligation or genuine desire? Obligation tends to tighten the body; desire softens it.

- Will this nourish me or deplete me?

- Is this aligned with my long-term values? Does it hold integrity with who I am becoming?

- Would I choose this if no one knew I was doing it? Or am I doing it to be seen, approved of, or validated?

4. Listen to your body's first reaction before your mind tries to rationalize the situation.

The more often you pause and check in before acting, the easier it becomes to recognize alignment in real time. Over time, this practice strengthens self-respect, deepens self-trust, and brings your life into greater coherence with your values and vision. Aligned actions then accumulate, building momentum so you can create a life that feels like you.

Journal Prompts

Notice

- How do you typically create or make decisions, from urgency or from presence? How does each feel in your body?

- Where does your life feel intentionally designed, and where does it feel inherited or automatic?

- Do you allow yourself to create without needing the result to prove anything? If so, how does your creativity flow differently?

Reflect

- What messages did you absorb growing up about success, achievement, or rest?

- When you hear the phrase "worthy life," what comes to mind? Do you imagine internal fullness or external validation?

- Where might you be chasing someone else's definition of success instead of honoring your own capacity?

Integrate

- What rewards do you currently use to soothe stress, and do they regulate or deplete you? What is one aligned reward that genuinely nourishes your nervous system?

- Is there one small, grounded choice you could make today that would better reflect your values?

Rewiring Your Outlook

I am the designer of a life that reflects my grounded worthiness.

Going Forward

As you move forward from this chapter, remember that designing a worthy life is not a dramatic overhaul. It is an accumulation of aligned choices, made from a regulated, grounded state. Each moment where you pause, check in with your body, soften urgency, or return to grounded worthiness becomes a quiet act of self-respect. These micro-moments build the foundation that reflects your truth rather than your wounds. Your life begins to take shape around who you are becoming rather than who you were taught to be.

Let your creative expression arise from this new foundation of safety and inner worth, and your decisions be shaped by your values and your vision be paced by your capacity. Allow yourself to receive the support, inspiration, and abundance that flows toward you when you no longer create from lack. You are choosing, expressing, and aligning rather than rushing, performing, and striving. These shifts are the architecture of the life you are designing.

Your worth does not come from what you produce, perform, or achieve. Your wealth is not measured by output, accomplishments, or approval. It comes from the inner resources that you cultivate: safety, presence, self-trust, grounded worthiness, joy, and alignment.

The next chapter explores the profound shift from defining yourself by your productivity to recognizing yourself as the source of creativity, wisdom, and meaning. You will reconnect with the inherent wealth that exists within you: the wealth of being you. This is the deep inner abundance that cannot be taken, diminished, or proven. Rather, it is remembered and embodied.

When you know *how* to create from a state of sufficiency, the next step is seeing *why* you can: This brings you home to yourself as the vessel, the place where ideas form, where intuition speaks, where guidance arises, and where your life is shaped from the inside out. Everything that you have healed so far has prepared you to hold this truth. Now, we step into it fully.

—

CHAPTER 19

THE WEALTH OF BEING YOU

Your value does not come from how much you produce, how much you achieve, or how much you give. And your worthiness is not earned through results. Your worth is inherent, and when you honor this truth, something profound shifts: You start respecting your capacity, honoring your limits, and choosing aligned opportunities, rather than defaulting to old patterns of overextension.

When you live as the vessel, your self-worth remains constant as it is not tied to your capacity or productivity. You live as the source of creativity, intuition, and soul-led expression, rather than as the product or the performance. You stop abandoning yourself for external validation, and begin choosing opportunities that respect your boundaries, values, and energy. Rest and nourishment become an essential part of your life rather than optional luxuries. You learn to protect your vessel with confidence, grounding into what strengthens you rather than what drains you. You can expand your capacity to receive life without proving your worth.

Signs That You Are Identifying with the End Product

You may be slipping back into product mode when:

- You fear losing momentum, so you avoid rest.
- You feel anxious when you're not producing or achieving.
- You measure your worth by your output.
- You say yes out of pressure, expectation, or fear, not desire.
- You override intuitive signals that it's time to pause.

These patterns often come from conditioning, trauma, or generational beliefs that would equate productivity with worthiness. Recognizing these patterns is a chance to recalibrate. You are the well, not the water drawn from it.

Redefining Success

We have been taught to associate thriving with relentless productivity, material achievement, and visible markers of success, often while standing on the shaky foundations of burnout, anxiety, and self-neglect. We push harder, even as our bodies beg us to slow down.

For many people, the misalignment comes from chasing someone else's version of success, a version built on comparison, social pressure, or internalized expectations. When you pursue goals because you feel that you should—in order to keep up with expectations, or because you fear falling behind—it becomes another form of people-pleasing. Or perhaps you think that if you have what someone else has, you will finally feel happy. Trying to keep up with an external version of success becomes a treadmill that never stops. It becomes a relentless proving ground that leads nowhere, as the bar keeps moving and the chase never ends, leaving you feeling exhausted, unfulfilled, and disconnected from yourself.

Soul-aligned success feels different. It feels nourishing, expansive, and deeply gratifying. It doesn't require contorting yourself to match someone else's vision, because it arises from your values, your energy, your desires, and your truth. Soul-aligned success means breaking generational patterns and choosing alignment over approval. You prioritize your peace, honoring your nervous system and resting without guilt. You live by your values, creating sustainably and cultivating joy.

Allow yourself to take the time to explore what success means to you, and ask yourself: *Is this an aligned and sustainable expression of me?* Soul-aligned goals will feel nourishing and fulfilling.

Aligned Goals versus Misaligned Goals

When your nervous system is dysregulated, goals tend to be misaligned, as they are coming from urgency, fear, comparison, or scarcity. Misaligned goals are disconnected from your values, and often feel draining and constricting. You end up sacrificing your relationships, time with friends and family, and your health in order to achieve the misaligned goals. You feel immense pressure and constantly behind, yet dread the work required to achieve, and you still look for external validation as a measure of success, feeling empty inside when you do meet your goals. When your goals are misaligned, you end up sacrificing your well-being to achieve them.

When your system is regulated, your goals flow from clarity, intuition, and possibility. Aligned goals feel clear, energizing, meaningful, coherent, and sustainable. Setting goals that honor your nervous system capacity creates momentum that is both attainable and sustainable.

Practices for Redesigning Your Definition of Success

Identify what truly matters. We did a values inventory practice in a previous chapter. Check in with your list. Does your current version of success align with your current values?

Check in with your body. When considering a new goal, pause and take notice of how your body feels when you think about it. Does it tighten or expand? Constrict or soften? Your body often knows before your mind does.

Build in recovery cycles. Success that is sustainable includes periods of rest, recalibration, and integration. This is not an optional luxury. Rather, it is a necessary part of the worthy life design.

Align your daily habits with your values. Alignment is lived through micro-choices. If you value health, how does that show up daily? If you value peace, how is that reflected in your schedule?

Celebrate the moments. When you reach a milestone, allow yourself to pause and acknowledge the moment. So many of us rush past accomplishment because we were conditioned to downplay ourselves, but celebration is a nervous system cue for safety and expansion.

The Daily Architecture of a Worthy Life

Embodied worthiness is not a mindset you think your way into. It is something you practice one moment at a time. A worthy life is not built through grand gestures, massive breakthroughs, or sudden reinventions. It is built through the quiet architecture of your days: the rhythms you keep, the habits you return to, the moments where you choose presence over pressure and nourishment over depletion.

When your nervous system has spent years in survival mode, your body must *experience* the truth of your worthiness repeatedly. That is why the daily architecture of your life matters. Your nervous system believes what is practiced. It is not about perfection; it is about consistency. Taking small, repeated actions will slowly change your internal landscape, creating conditions for your nervous system to thrive.

The day-to-day reality of a worthy life means that you are paced at your capacity, with moments of rest woven into your routine. You make choices that support your values and decisions that reinforce self-respect. Perhaps you practice sensory experiences that cue safety and rituals that remind your body that you matter.

Your body responds instantly to sensory cues, and small shifts like these can quietly transform your baseline: soft lighting in the morning, calming scents that cue relaxation, warm drinks that ground you, textures that soothe and comfort, and music that feels regulating. These cues collectively teach your body that daily life is not a threat, that you are safe enough to soften, and safe enough to receive.

Rituals are simply routines done with intention. They are tiny pockets of reverence woven through the day, becoming anchors that stabilize the body and remind you of who you are becoming. Here are some examples:

- A three-breath pause before you transition to a new task
- A noon check-in: What do I need?
- Stepping outside for sunlight
- Stretching your neck between emails
- Lighting a candle before journaling
- Placing a hand on your heart before bed and offering gratitude

These micro-moments reinforce internal safety and accumulate into a life that feels calm, coherent, and aligned with your worth. Designing a worthy life is designing your *days* to support the version of you that you are becoming. When your daily architecture shifts, your identity follows. A felt sense of worthiness emerges gradually as the nervous system experiences rest without guilt, pleasure without fear, expression without self-abandonment, boundaries without panic, and joy without waiting for the other shoe to drop. You shift from *I know that I matter*, to *My body can feel that I matter*.

The Nervous System & Money Narratives

Money wounds are rarely about money itself. Often, they are nervous system stories that are based on inherited beliefs, emotional imprints, and survival strategies passed down through families, cultures, or past versions of ourselves. Other times they are rooted in deep-seated fears or limiting perceptions.

Most people don't realize that receiving, whether it's money, rest, love, support, or recognition, is a physiological experience long before it becomes a financial one. If receiving has ever felt unsafe, unfamiliar, or forbidden, the nervous system will unconsciously resist it. This is why someone can want abundance yet freeze when opportunities arrive, or they might work tirelessly but sabotage success at the last moment. Earning more can feel overwhelming rather than exciting.

These are not failures of discipline or mindset; they are nervous system responses shaped by stories that end up blocking abundance. When you see yourself as *the vessel*, not *the product*, your relationship with receiving naturally transforms, as you stop tying your value to your output. You shift your belief that you must earn, justify, or prove your worthiness to receive, and slowly, abundance begins to feel safe.

Inherited Blocks Around Money, Success & Receiving

Below are some common narratives that people can unconsciously absorb. They are stories, not truths, but they end up shaping what the nervous system perceives as safe.

> *Money is hard to come by.*
>
> *People with money are greedy and selfish.*
>
> *If I slow down, I'll fall behind.*
>
> *I'll be hated or resented if I succeed.*
>
> *If I receive too much, something bad will happen.*
>
> *I'm not ready yet. I need to fix myself first.*
>
> *If I try and fail, it will confirm that I'm not enough.*
>
> *Desiring abundance is selfish and superficial.*
>
> *I should be sharing my gifts for free.*
>
> *It's not spiritual to want wealth.*

These narratives become somatic patterns whenever money, growth, or expansion enters the conversation. They manifest through tightness in the chest, a clenched jaw, racing thoughts, hesitancy, procrastination, self-sabotage, and complete avoidance. But once you recognize these money and success narratives for what they are, you reclaim your power to shift them, and receiving becomes possible again. You approach abundance not from urgency, fear, or proving, but from a grounded sense of worth. You stop trying to earn your value and start allowing yourself to receive.

As you loosen your grip on old money narratives, you clear the path for soul-aligned success, the kind that supports your nervous system rather than overwhelms it. Instead of chasing someone else's version of success, you shape a life that honors your values, your capacity, and your inner truth.

This is the essence of nervous system wealth: the ability to hold safety, sufficiency, and self-worth as your baseline. From here, we move into designing your life from alignment, choosing goals, habits, and environments that support the vessel you are becoming.

Reframing the Blocks: Shifting Money Narratives Through Nervous System Safety

Money blocks are rarely just beliefs. Rather, they are protective patterns wired into the nervous system. As we heal, we think new thoughts—and we teach the body a new truth.

Reframing is the process of first identifying the outdated story. Then you give it attention with the aim of understanding the protective function that it once served. This opens the opportunity to choose a new narrative that supports safety, possibility, and self-worth.

Here are examples of common money or success narratives, paired with nervous-system-aligned reframes:

Block: "Rich people are selfish and corrupt. Money changes people."
Reframe: "Money amplifies what already exists. In aligned, compassionate hands, money becomes a tool for healing, generosity, and impact."

Block: "Money doesn't grow on trees."

Reframe: "Abundance is all around me, in opportunities, creativity, connection, and support."

Block: "I should just be grateful for what I have."

Reframe: "Gratitude and desire can coexist. I can appreciate my life while also expanding into what I'm becoming."

Block: "I'm bad with money. I can't be trusted to manage more."

Reframe: "Skills can be learned. I can grow my financial confidence one small step at a time."

Block: "Good things don't last."

Reframe: "Stability grows through consistency, self-trust, and nervous system support."

Block: "Something bad always happens when things are going well."

Reframe: "I can let safety feel familiar. Not everything has to be balanced by struggle."

Why Reframing Matters

Reframing is not an instant fix. It is a practice of rewriting internal stories so your body can experience abundance without bracing against it. Each new narrative offers your nervous system a fresh cue of safety:

> *Expansion is safe.*
>
> *Good things are allowed to stay.*
>
> *I'm worthy of receiving without overworking.*
>
> *I can create a future that feels nourishing, not overwhelming.*

The Receiving Threshold: How Much Can Your Nervous System Hold?

Every person has a receiving threshold, an internal limit of how much goodness, support, abundance, love, success, rest, joy, or ease your nervous system feels safe holding. Your receiving threshold is shaped by childhood conditioning, generational narratives, trauma imprints, attachment patterns, past experiences of loss or disappointment, cultural messages about what you "deserve," as well as your nervous system states.

In survival mode, even positive experiences can feel threatening. Joy is unfamiliar, receiving feels dangerous, and success is overwhelming. So the body does what it has learned to do: it constricts, sabotages, and shuts the door before too much good gets in. It is not because you do not deserve it; rather, it is because your nervous system has not yet learned how to hold it. When your body shifts to this constricting mode, it is at its receiving threshold.

How the Receiving Threshold Shows Up

Common ways a limited receiving threshold appears:

Joy feels suspicious or short-lived. You anticipate the crash. You wait for something to go wrong. You mentally prepare for loss.

You can receive a little . . . but not too much. A small compliment is fine, but a big opportunity feels terrifying. A small gift feels safe, but a major blessing makes you want to hide.

You sabotage right when things start going well. You pick a fight. You procrastinate. You back out, or you shut down.

You say *no* to help, support, or rest. You cling to independence because support feels unfamiliar. You fear being indebted or judged. You feel guilty resting or receiving care.

You shrink or play small around others. You hide what you want and downplay your success because visibility feels unsafe.

Your body contracts when you receive. Your body reacts physically, where you experience a tight chest, clenched jaw, or stomach drop. You may also feel restlessness or an urge to flee. The body is simply communicating that it doesn't yet know how to hold more.

Why the Receiving Threshold Exists

The nervous system prefers what is familiar, even if the familiar is painful. You may have grown up with unpredictability, scarcity, emotional instability, criticism, shame, pressure, guilt, never having enough, or being told you didn't deserve more. Because of this, your body learned that expansion is unsafe and receiving is risky. So when abundance arrives in any form, your system responds as if you're in danger. This is why affirmation alone can't fix receiving wounds. The mind may want to expand, but the nervous system contracts.

How to Expand Your Receiving Threshold

You don't force expansion; you slowly and gently teach your body that receiving is safe. Here are the core pillars:

Micro-Moments of Receiving

Each tiny moment tells your system: *It is safe to let good things in.*
Start very small:

- Accept the compliment.
- Let someone hold the door.
- Allow yourself a five-minute rest.
- Receive help without immediately giving back.
- Say "thank you" without deflecting.

Somatic Softening

Cue safety in the body when receiving:

- Unclench your jaw.
- Soften your belly and breathe deeper.
- Relax your shoulders.
- Open your palms and place a hand on your heart.

These signals complete the receiving loop.

Practice Holding Good Things Without Bracing

When something good happens, take a moment to pause before the mind rushes in with fear or withdrawal. Feel the goodness in the body and observe it for a few seconds. This strengthens your capacity.

Rewrite the receiving narrative. Gently reframe old beliefs: *It's safe to let this in. Good things are allowed to stay. I don't need to earn what's meant for me. My worth isn't tied to output. Receiving is an expression of self-respect.*

Celebrate small wins. Your nervous system learns through repetition. The more you allow yourself to receive small amounts of good, the larger your threshold becomes.

Regulate before you expand. A regulated system can hold more joy. Expansion without regulation feels like a threat. Find safety for your nervous system first, then expand.

Track the edge. Be mindful of how much goodness you can tolerate before your body contracts. This awareness lets you gently increase your capacity over time.

The Receiving Threshold & Abundance

When you expand your ability to hold goodness, you can naturally:

- Receive more
- Feel safer with success
- Stop sabotaging
- Allow support
- Rest without guilt
- Expand without fear
- Trust yourself
- Trust the path

This is a pillar of nervous system wealth: abundance that feels safe, sustainable, and rooted, allowing you to design a life based on expansion rather than survival.

Manifestation & Raising Your Vibration

Manifestation is a byproduct of nervous system regulation. You do not manifest from your mind; you manifest from your nervous system's feeling of safety. If everything is energy, including your thoughts, emotions, and choices, then the frequency you hold shapes what you attract. Lower vibrational states like fear, scarcity, shame, and self-doubt are not moral failings; they are signs of a dysregulated nervous system. They are survival states, not spiritual deficiencies.

As you begin healing, regulating, and grounding, your vibration naturally lifts.

safety → gratitude
presence → clarity
contentment → possibility
authenticity → expansion
self-worth → attraction

Activities that leave you feeling joy and appreciation, and thoughts that are expansive and creative, will naturally raise your vibrational state. When you can maintain a generally positive outlook, then you are sustaining a path that leads to the life that you want to live. This is why nervous system work is foundational in manifestation. You cannot magnetize a life of joy while your body is still bracing for threat. You cannot call in abundance while your subconscious beliefs are blocking your capacity to receive. Raising your vibration is not about forcing positivity; it is about creating internal safety so higher states can emerge naturally.

Gratitude becomes a key part of this process. It literally shifts your nervous system toward safety, softens threat responses, and opens your body to receive. Remember, gratitude is not about denying hardship, it is about acknowledging goodness even amid challenge. The more moments of grateful awareness you accumulate, the more your vibration stabilizes, and the more receptive you become to aligned possibilities.

Manifestation becomes easier when:

- Your nervous system feels safe.
- Your self-worth is intact.
- You are regulated enough to visualize clearly.
- You believe you deserve what you desire.
- You feel content in the present moment.

Contentment creates a stable foundation. Gratitude raises the frequency. Presence focuses the energy. Self-worth holds the container open. This is manifestation from the body, not from force.

"Faking it until you make it" can only go so far if your nervous system is still in survival mode or if inner limitations are still active beneath the surface. Affirmations can help, not because they force change, but because they gently rewire the stories you tell yourself. Just as negative words can shape your identity, positive words, repeated with safety, consistency, and compassion, can reshape your inner landscape. This is nervous-system-informed manifestation: grounded, embodied, sustainable.

The Wealth of Being You

Your inner abundance, found in safety, alignment, presence, and joy, is your truest form of wealth. The wealth of being you is not something you earn, build, or prove. It is something you uncover that trauma, conditioning, and survival mode may have obscured, but never erased.

When you heal your nervous system, your self-worth rises from the inside out. You move through the world with a deeper connection to who you are, rather than who you were taught to be.

This kind of wealth is internal, embodied, and unshakable. It cannot be taken from you, because it is not dependent on achievement, financial markers, or the approval of others. It is rooted in alignment, integrity, and nervous system safety.

When you live from this place, you trust yourself, you honor your limits, and you follow your inner compass. Your boundaries strengthen, and your capacity for joy, rest, and receiving expands.

For much of your life, you may have been taught that wealth equals money, accomplishments, milestones, and an accumulation of material possessions. But when your nervous system is dysregulated, even these achievements can feel hollow. You may reach a milestone but still feel a sense of lack. You may experience financial stability yet remain on edge, waiting for everything to fall apart, because no external gain can create an internal sense of safety.

Nervous system wealth changes everything. When your body learns safety, you can finally experience freedom rather than pressure, joy rather than vigilance, rooted worthiness rather than striving, and presence rather than future fear. You become rooted within yourself, grounded in your values, and resilient in the face of uncertainty. You no longer chase validation, remembering that you were always worthy of love, rest, and abundance.

The wealth of being you is an inner state of ease and alignment. You do not have to earn it. You simply reclaim what has always been yours.

This kind of wealth shows up as deep self-acceptance and trust in your inner voice. You are free from comparison and feel safe to expand without fear. You experience joy that feels stable and alignment that feels natural. You have the capacity to rest without guilt.

This is wealth that nourishes and lasts, and it cannot be taken from you. It is wealth that exists independently of your circumstances. When you root into who you truly are, you no longer chase life, you co-create it. You stop striving to be the product and begin honoring yourself as the vessel, the sacred container through which inspiration, intuition, and creation flow. You become the source, not the performance. You become the artist, not the output, and that is the wealth of being you.

Nervous System Reset: Vibrational Matches

We've explored throughout this book how your thoughts, emotions, and the state of your nervous system shape what you allow and attract into your life. This exercise helps you identify where your current vibration may be out of alignment with your desires. Rather than chase or force outcomes, you can reflect on where your energy is mismatched with your true desires.

You are not failing to manifest; your body may simply not feel safe holding the emotional frequency of what you want. If joy, abundance, love, or ease feel unfamiliar or overwhelming, your nervous system may unconsciously block them, even if you consciously want them.

The Practice

This practice helps you gently shift your vibration into a state your nervous system can recognize, trust, and eventually embody.

1. Find a quiet, comfortable space. Take several slow grounding breaths, letting your shoulders soften and your breath deepen.

2. Identify your current vibration. Ask yourself honestly: What emotional or energetic state am I most often living in? For example:

scarcity, urgency, doubt, overwhelm, peace, gratitude, hope, or joy. There is no wrong answer. This is awareness, not judgment.

3. Identify your desired vibration. Now ask yourself: Is the state I spend most of my time in the same state I want to be vibrating from? If not, name your desired frequency. Here are more examples: calm, grounded, confident, or abundant. Now close your eyes and imagine what it would feel like to embody that vibration.

Get very specific here:

Where are you and what are you doing?

What are you wearing?

Who are you with?

Do you live differently? Move differently? Speak differently?

What words arise in this frequency?

How does your body feel when you imagine it?

Let your nervous system feel the possibility.

4. Compare the two states. Notice the difference between your current vibration and your desired vibration. Is there a small or large gap between them? Does the desired state feel safe in your body, or does it bring up tension and resistance? This reflection is essential as it reveals the places where your nervous system is still protecting you.

5. Introduce micro-moments of the desired vibration. Once you've identified where you want your vibration to be, you can introduce micro-moments into your life to show safety to your nervous system and start bridging the gap between where you are and where you want to be. Find more ways to bring that vibration into your life in small ways.

Gentle Ways to Invite Alignment

- If you desire joy, invite more laughter into your day.

- If you desire gratitude, pause to offer small moments of thanks.

- If you desire peace, add brief grounding breaths throughout your day.

- If you desire abundance, practice receiving small acts of kindness without guilt.

Over time, these gentle practices shift your energetic baseline. Rather than pretending or forcing a new vibration, you are training your body to feel safe in that state. Then you can continue to expand the practice, bringing more moments of safety in. As your vibration shifts, you naturally attract and allow experiences, opportunities, and relationships that match this new frequency. Eventually your new vibration goal becomes your new state of being.

Journal Prompts

Notice

- When you imagine earning more or receiving more, what sensations arise in your body?

- What happens in your body when you imagine being more visible or expanded? Does expansion feel safe, overwhelming, or somewhere in between?

Reflect

- What were you taught about money and receiving growing up?

- Are you afraid of surpassing someone you love or outgrowing familiar dynamics? How would your social circle and family react if you suddenly had lots of money? How does that make you feel?

- Do you believe you must work hard or suffer to deserve success?

Integrate

- What would it feel like to receive with ease rather than effort?

- Is there a new narrative about money or success you want to practice moving forward?

- What is one small way you could practice receiving, whether it is support, praise, money, or help, without immediately proving your worth or reciprocating?

Rewiring Your Outlook

My value lies in my being, not what I produce.

Going Forward

As you move beyond this chapter, remember that you are the vessel through which your work, your relationships, and your creativity flow. Your worth has never come from what you produce or how perfectly you perform. This chapter has taught you to slow down, take care, redefine success on your own terms, and treat yourself as the sacred vessel you truly are.

From this foundation of nervous system safety and self-worth, you become capable of creating a life that feels deeply aligned, sustainable, and fulfilling—not because you push harder, but because you are finally designing from grounded worthiness. When you honor your limits, nourish your body, clarify your values, and choose soul-aligned success rather than externally defined achievement, you reclaim your energy and your power.

The next chapter invites you into the next phase of this work. If the previous chapters helped you clear the noise, regulate your system, and reconnect with your inner compass, this chapter is where you shape the path ahead with intention. Designing forward is not about rigid goal setting, forcing outcomes, or mapping your life through hustle. It is about learning to design your future from your body, from alignment, and from the version of you that is rooted into embodied worthiness.

We will explore how to make decisions from sufficiency rather than scarcity, how to choose goals that match your nervous system's current capacity, how to create micro-shifts that compound into meaningful change, and how to build a life that supports you rather than drains you. Designing forward is the natural next step in your evolution, a gentle but powerful movement toward the life you're meant to live, crafted from a deep sense of inner wealth.

———

CHAPTER 20

DESIGNING FORWARD

Designing forward is the point in your journey where healing begins to transform into conscious creation. You are no longer reacting to life from old wounds or survival responses. You are no longer waiting for permission, approval, or the right circumstances. You are the architect, moving with intention and planning from regulation and alignment. You are steady, grounded, and attuned to your capacity, softly expanding to your envisioned future. This is where your healing becomes your compass.

Nervous-System-Aligned Goal Setting

Most people set goals from pressure, fear of falling behind, comparison, or internalized expectations. These goals may look impressive on paper, but they rarely feel good in the body, and even when achieved, they do not create fulfillment. Designing forward means setting goals that align with your values, match your nervous system's actual capacity, and honor the pace at which your body feels safe to expand. This is how you create a future that is sustainable, not stressful.

Capacity-Based Planning

Traditional goal setting often ignores an important variable, your body's capacity. Your capacity can depend on your current nervous system state, levels of rest, your bandwidth, your obligations, as well as your baseline stress load. When capacity is low, even a small goal feels impossible. When capacity is nourished, creative action becomes fluid and expansive.

Checking in with your capacity before setting goals creates alignment rather than overwhelm. It prevents the cycle of overcommitting, which is often followed by burnout, shame, then shutting down.

Using Values & Boundaries as Design Tools

Your goals should be shaped by what matters to you, not what you think should matter, and not what looks impressive on the outside.

Ask yourself:

Does this goal honor my top values?

Does this require me to violate my boundaries?

Does this support the life I actually want to live?

Does it feel nourishing to work toward this, or depleting?

When your values and boundaries guide your future, you no longer chase goals that do not belong to you. You create from authenticity, not obligation.

Distinguishing Desire from Pressure

The nervous system feels the difference instantly. Desire that is deeply aligned feels like a gentle pull forward. There is clarity and ease. You feel curious, excited, and open. These are all signs that your nervous system is ready for expansion and that your dreams are safe to pursue.

Pressure, on the other hand, feels like urgency, guilt, and comparison. You carry the energy of "I should" and are afraid of falling behind. Take notice of how your body reacts. If a goal collapses your shoulders, constricts your chest, or spikes adrenaline, it is likely based on pressure, not desire. Designing forward means choosing goals your body can say *yes* to.

Pacing That Honors Regulation

Pacing is how you signal to your nervous system that expansion is safe. You don't sprint toward your future until you collapse. You take steady, sustainable steps that keep your system in its window of tolerance, hovering in a comfortable state of taking action.

Aligned pacing considers what your capacity is from day to day and knowing when to take a break. You realize that resting will not affect your momentum if your goal is deeply aligned. When you pace yourself with compassion, you build a life you do not have to recover from.

You are not designing forward from adrenaline anymore. You are designing forward from rooted worthiness and self-trust. This is the foundation of long-term expansion:

- Goals that feel safe in the body
- Actions that match your capacity
- Values that align with who you want to be
- Pacing that keeps you regulated

Personal Responsibility: The Shift from Passive to Active Creation

Personal responsibility is not self-blame; rather it is self-ownership. It is the moment you recognize that your life is shaped by your choices, your patterns, your boundaries, and your willingness to change. When you take personal responsibility, you are taking full accountability for your words, actions, emotions, and reactions. You accept that the consequences of your decisions are the result of your choices, and so you step out of the role of the victim and into the role of the creator. You stop blaming other people and circumstances that are outside of your control. You no longer wait for other people or circumstances to change, or for someone to rescue you. Life stops happening to you, and you begin participating in it from a place of empowered choice. You become the change that you want to see.

It means:

- You take accountability for your actions and reactions.
- You acknowledge the consequences of your choices.
- You stop waiting for someone else to rescue you.
- You make decisions instead of deferring them.
- You build the life you want instead of hoping someone builds it for you.

Your deeper sense of self-awareness is the foundation upon which taking personal responsibility becomes possible. It is one of the pillars of personal growth and development, and it leads to the possibility of conscious creation.

Clean Up Your Thoughts to Clean Up Your Energy

When a thought carries fear, self-criticism, resentment, or scarcity, your energy contracts. Your nervous system shifts toward defense. Your perspective narrows. When a thought carries clarity, sufficiency, curiosity, or compassion, your energy expands. Your body opens. Your capacity grows. Designing forward requires this subtle practice of noticing which thoughts drain your energy and which thoughts restore it. As your thoughts become cleaner, lighter, and more aligned, your energy naturally follows, and your actions reflect your expansion rather than your wounds.

Language as Nervous System Design: The Spells We Speak

As we design forward, one of the most subtle yet powerful tools we have is language. Up to this point in the book, we've worked on grounding the body, honoring capacity, redefining success, and making aligned choices. But those shifts can only take root when the way we speak to ourselves supports them. This is why language becomes part of the design process. The words we use and the stories we tell ourselves can quietly activate survival mode or softly guide you back into regulation. Every phrase becomes a signal. Your body listens to what you say and responds as if the words are true.

We often speak in ways that reinforce urgency:

> *I should be further along.*

> *I have to fix this.*

> *There's not enough time.*

> *I need to get my life together.*

Your body hears these statements as cues of danger, and your nervous system shifts into pressure and urgency. The shoulders tense, the jaw tightens, and breath becomes shallow. Suddenly you're designing from fear and self-pressure rather than from grounded clarity.

Language can also become a form of self-abandonment: saying *yes* when you mean *no*; downplaying your needs; apologizing even if it is unnecessary; or speaking about yourself through a lens inherited from others rather than from your truth. But when you consciously shift your language, even slightly, you create micro-moments of alignment. Language then becomes one of the most accessible forms of nervous system design. Think of the phrases you repeat as spells. Every one of them shapes your inner architecture.

Reframed Phrases: From Survival Mode to Regulation

Below are some gentle alternatives to the most common dysregulating phrases:

From Pressure → To Choice

"I should do this." → "I choose to do this because . . . "

"I have to." → "I'm deciding to."

"I don't have a choice." → "I'm choosing the option that supports me most."

From Overwhelm → To Agency

"This is too much." → "I can take this one step at a time."

"I can't handle this." → "I can pause and resource."

"Everything is chaotic." → "My next step is clear."

From Scarcity → To Sufficiency

"I don't have time." → "I'm not prioritizing that right now."

"I'm behind." → "I'm moving at the right pace for me."

"I need to earn rest." → "My body is worthy of rest right now."

From Self-Doubt → To Self-Respect

"I'm failing." → "I'm learning and expanding."

"I always mess things up." → "I'm practicing."

"I don't know what I'm doing." → "I can figure this out step by step."

From Urgency → To Safety

"This has to work." → "I'm open to the next aligned step."

"I need to fix this now." → "I can pause before I decide."

"I'm running out of time." → "I can move slowly enough to think clearly."

From Self Abandonment → To Boundaries

"It's fine—I'll handle it." → "Let me check in with my capacity first."

"I don't want to be a burden." → "My needs matter too."

"It's not a big deal." → "My needs are valid."

"I'll just take care of it." → "I deserve support too."

"I'll just push through." → "Pushing won't serve me—I can pause."

From Fear of Visibility → To Rooted Expression

"People will judge me." → "My voice is allowed here."

"I'm not ready." → "I can begin small and steady."

"What if I say the wrong thing?" → "I can speak from truth and self-trust."

Your language shapes how your nervous system experiences expansion. As you design your future, language becomes both compass and anchor. You don't need perfect phrasing, just honest, gentle, regulating language that aligns with the person you are becoming.

Vibrational & Energetic Alignment

It is important to seek out energetic and vibrational matches, as being in an aligned environment gives your nervous system the safety cues that it needs. In order to continue fostering growth and expansion, you need to be in an environment that supports safety, expansion, joy, and possibility.

As you heal, your energy shifts and your frequency rises. Your standards sharpen, and suddenly, things that once felt normal begin to feel heavy. You may find that certain people, places, and habits are no longer a match for you. This is nervous system evolution. As your frequency shifts, there will also be a shift in what feels aligned to you.

As your system recalibrates, you may notice:

- Habits you once relied on now feel misaligned.

- Conversations rooted in drama feel draining.

- Emotional eating or impulse behaviors no longer soothe.

- Friendships built on shared wounds begin to dissolve.

- Environments you once tolerated suddenly feel loud, chaotic, or suffocating.

This growth and healing process changes what you are a match for, and misaligned frequencies become harder to sit with. Bonds that you made based on old wounds will dissolve as you heal that wound. Even habits can dissolve. When you no longer need to soothe a wound with a certain habit, for example emotional eating, then that habit will no longer align with your life, and you stop doing it. Remember, it's okay if some things no longer resonate with you; it is a sign that you are making progress on your healing journey. This isn't judgment. It is energetic alignment.

When you experience growth and healing, your values, perspectives, and general outlook on life will change, and you will naturally move away from the people, situations, and habits that no longer align. We are all on our own healing journey, and it is a path that we must walk alone and at our own pace. Some people are not ready to heal. They are not ready for change. Try to hold grace and compassion for them rather than judgment.

Practices for Designing Forward

At this point in the book, you are thinking about what you want your future to look like, and you are making conscious choices to get there. You are rooted in self-worth and nervous system safety and pacing yourself based on your true capacity. Your choices are intentional, hovering in a state of comfortable action. You are no longer procrastinating or self-sabotaging your dreams, but you are also not pushing yourself beyond your capacity. Your growth feels both aligned and sustainable. You are using your inner compass to align with your values and your vision of the future. You are checking in with your body to make sure that your actions stay with your capacity, signaling to your body that expansion is safe so that you can continue to grow.

As you allow yourself to design the future you desire, sketch your vision: Imagine your life one, three, or five years from now. What do your days look like? What habits define your life? What relationships or environments nourish you? Be specific, not just about what you want, but how it feels.

Every vision requires energy, time, and nervous system bandwidth. When you consider your capacity, ask yourself what you can realistically hold right now. Let this reflection be a guide.

Once you have an idea of what feels both realistic and aligned, then you can break big goals into clear, gentle steps. Use micro goals, soft deadlines, and compassionate pacing. This is how you prevent overwhelm and build self-trust. I like the SMART strategy, but find what resonates with you.

SMART goals are a simple but powerful framework for bringing clarity and structure to your desires. The acronym stands for Specific, Measurable, Achievable, Relevant, and Time-bound, five qualities that help transform vague intentions into grounded, embodied action.

When filtered through the lens of nervous system safety, SMART goals become even more supportive: "Specific" helps eliminate vagueness and reduce overwhelm. "Measurable" gives your brain and body tangible evidence of progress, showing your body that the small wins are safe to receive. "Achievable" ensures your goals match your current capacity and pacing needs. "Relevant" keeps you aligned with your values and vision of the future instead of external pressure. "Time-bound" gives your nervous system gentle structure, eliminating the feeling that you need to rush forward with a sense of urgency. This framework helps you pace your growth, build self-trust, and design a path forward that honors both your vision and your body.

Remember to review and reflect on your goals on a regular basis. Designing forward is not linear. You will adjust and evolve, and your desires will shift as you heal. Reflection keeps you aligned rather than forcing goals that are no longer a match.

Finding Peace with Your Past

You cannot change the past, but you can change how you look at the past. You can shift away from shame and regret and stop thinking in terms of "if only" or "what if." Instead, you can embrace the idea that every moment of your past has led you to this exact moment in time, and trust that you are precisely where you need to be. You begin to see that every difficult, messy, and painful moment shaped your strength, every mistake taught you something essential, every detour led you here, and every season was preparing you for this version of yourself.

You don't have to love the past, but you can stop fighting it. Acceptance regulates the nervous system, anchors you into the present, and opens the road ahead. When you can accept the place that you are in now, you are more able to trust the path forward. Leaning into that trust can help you feel safer in the unknowns of the future, which in turn keeps our nervous system regulated.

Habit Stacking for the Future You

Our lives are shaped by the habits we repeat, and often one behavior triggers another. For example, snacking mindlessly whenever you watch TV, or reaching for sugar whenever you feel stressed. But instead of trying to break habits with force, we can replace them with aligned stacks that support our growth and well-being. Over time, these tiny shifts compound into massive change.

Here is what a healthy habit stack might look like:

> *When I feel stressed, I take three grounding breaths.*
>
> *After I brush my teeth, I do one minute of facial massage.*
>
> *When I feel overwhelmed, I step outside for fresh air.*

Nervous System Reset: Vision Embodiment & Design

The Vision Embodiment Practice teaches both your mind and your body to hold the frequency of the future you desire. Instead of imagining change that feels vague and distant, this practice helps you to embody the emotional and energetic state of your future self in the present moment. When the body learns that expansion is safe, it becomes easier to receive what you desire rather than chase it.

When you repeatedly visualize the details of your future, how you live, how you feel, how you move through your day, you gently teach your nervous system that the future is both safe and possible. From that place, your desired reality becomes a vibrational match rather than an aspirational idea.

The Practice

This practice can be done as a guided meditation, as a journaling ritual, or paired with a vision board for a more tactile, visual experience. Whether you are using imagery, words, or physical symbols, the goal is the same: to allow your nervous system to become familiar with the life and vibration you are calling in through the felt experience of that future self.

1. Find a quiet, comfortable place where you won't be interrupted. Sit or lie down in a position where your body can soften, and take a few deep, grounding breaths.

2. When you are ready, close your eyes and bring to mind a future version of yourself, one who is living in nervous system regulation and in alignment with your values and desires.

3. Observe the details with curiosity:

- Where does this version of you live? Who are you spending your time with?

- What does a typical day feel like? What does a typical day look like? Get very specific.

- How does this future version of you move through the day? What pace and energy?

- What do self-care, self-talk, self-worth, and self-confidence look like?

4. Now imagine stepping directly into that version of yourself and feeling what it is like to inhabit that reality right now. Imagine that you are already living that life. Notice the posture and breath of this future self, and any sensations of ease, confidence, clarity, or calm. Notice what expands inside you when you imagine being that person. Let the feeling become familiar and allow it to saturate your body, anchoring it into your nervous system.

5. Stay with these sensations for as long as you wish and remember how it feels to be living as this new version of yourself. This felt experience and embodied frequency is what you will want to repeatedly revisit.

Over time, it becomes your baseline, allowing you to draw in opportunities and experiences that resonate with this state of being. Practice becoming the version of you who can hold what you desire. This will allow you to become the vibrational match that you need to be in order to manifest the life that you want.

Nervous System Reset Part Two: Vision Board Ritual

A vision board may seem like a simple creative project, but it can also be a powerful nervous system practice. When your desires are expressed visually, your body receives a cue of possibility. Vision boards remind you to work on embodying the future that you desire, shifting your nervous system from striving into receiving.

The idea is to have a collection of words, pictures, and symbols that you associate with what you want more of in your life. This practice brings together intention, imagery, nervous system safety, and aligned manifestation. Because you've already clarified your values, boundaries, and aligned actions in previous chapters, this exercise becomes the next layer: visually shaping what you want more of in your life.

Supplies

- A poster board, corkboard, large sheet of paper, or notebook page

- Magazines, catalogs, printed images

- Scissors, glue, tape, or pushpins

- Markers, pens, paint, stickers

- Words or phrases you've written yourself

- Natural elements: leaves, petals, feathers, pressed flowers

- Ambiance: soft music, candle, warm beverage, cozy blanket

The Practice

1. Gather your materials and create an environment that feels grounding. The goal is to design your board from embodied worthiness and nervous system safety, creating a sensory collage of what your body deeply desires.

2. Select images that feel both safe and aligned. Leaf through magazines or scroll through printed images. As you do this, pause and check in with your body: Does this image feel expanding or constricting? Does it feel safe for my nervous system? Does this belong to my vision, or is it borrowed from comparison or cultural pressure?

Choose items that evoke warmth, curiosity, safety, and possibility, not anything you feel that you should choose based on external pressures or expectations. Let deep alignment guide you as you gather words, phrases, and images.

If you want a waterfront home, find an image of a shoreline that you like, or a picture of your dream home. If you want a healthier lifestyle, choose visuals that will motivate you to make those changes that support your health. Maybe that means making nourishing meals or adding in more movement. If you want to publish a book, choose images that spark creativity and inspire you to write.

3. Arrange the images intuitively. Spread your images on the table so that you can see them all, then arrange them without overthinking. There is no wrong way to do this. Place them in a way that feels aesthetically pleasing. Some people might want more structure, while others may want more of a collage layout. Let the board feel coherent, calming, and grounded, not stressful and overwhelming.

4. Secure and finalize. When your arrangement feels right, glue or tape the images down. Then add words, phrases, or affirmations. Include your values if you want them woven in visually. You can add symbols of nature or texture if that supports your sensory experience.

5. Embodied visualization. Sit with your finished board for a moment and let it land in your nervous system. Imagine yourself already experiencing the things that are on your vision board and try to embody that feeling of you having already arrived where you want to go. How does your body feel when you imagine these things already unfolding?

6. Display with intention. Place your vision board somewhere you will encounter it on a regular basis. This might be near your desk or on a closet door. You can even take a picture of it and use it as a background on your phone or laptop. Let it be a gentle reminder of your vision of the future. This way you are letting your nervous system get accustomed to a new level of safety and possibility.

Journal Prompts

Notice

- How do you know when your capacity is being honored versus overridden? What signals does your body give you?

- What language do you use most often that activates urgency or self-pressure? What phrases soften you instead?

- What does "designing forward" feel like in your body compared to striving or pushing?

Reflect

- Where in your life are you currently designing from desire, and where might pressure still be shaping your goals?

- Are there people, environments, or habits you have outgrown? What sensations arise when you imagine releasing them?

- When you reflect on your past, can you see where past challenges have strengthened you, taught you something essential, and prepared you for this version of yourself?

Integrate

- What is one experience you want to intentionally design more of in this season in your life? What is one you are ready to reduce or release?

- Imagine expanding into new environments, hobbies, or relationships that feel more aligned. What small step could you take to move toward one of these new experiences?

Rewiring Your Outlook

I design my future with embodied worth.

Going Forward

Designing forward is the moment where healing becomes movement. You are no longer operating from urgency, fear, or old patterns. You are choosing with intention. Every aligned decision, every micro-moment, every boundary honored becomes evidence to your nervous system that expansion is safe. You are learning to create from clarity, presence, and aligned desire, not from pressure, overwhelm, and obligation.

Your life begins to shift as your vibration shifts. Your habits become more nourishing. Your environment becomes more aligned. Your actions begin to match the person you are becoming. As you continue designing forward, trust yourself enough to go slow, honor your capacity, and let alignment, not adrenaline, set your pace. The life you are building is sustainable because it is rooted in who you truly are.

The next chapter gathers everything you have learned and presents it not as a checklist to master, but as a lived rhythm that now belongs to you. Integration is the gentle weaving of safety, self-worth, aligned action, and embodied presence into the fabric of your everyday life. It is the recognition that your growth is not a single breakthrough, but an ongoing relationship with yourself.

As you move into this final chapter, you are stepping into a deeper embodiment of who you have become and who you are continuing to rise into.

—

CHAPTER 21

INTEGRATION
Living the Work

Take a moment to recognize the courage that was required of you to do this deep level of self-exploration and healing. Allow the recognition of the journey that you have gone through. Self-exploration is by no means easy, so give yourself a hug or a pat on the back.

You have traveled through awareness, healing, reconnection, nervous system safety, visibility, rooted worthiness, and aligned creation. Now comes the most important part of the journey, integration, where the inner work you have done becomes the outer life. It is where practices become patterns, and patterns become identity. Your values and your choices move in the same direction rooted in embodied worthiness.

In this final chapter, we anchor everything you've learned into a lived experience. We explore how to weave together the entire journey and map how to bring these tools into daily life, how to sustain this regulated way of being, and how to continue growing without abandoning yourself. Integration is the ongoing commitment to live as the version of you who is rooted, present, and aligned. This chapter brings all the threads together so you can step fully into the life you desire.

Living the Work, Becoming the Work

Integration is where everything you have learned becomes a way of life. Nervous system wealth is not an endpoint or achievement; it is a lifelong practice. These practices are an ongoing choice to return to yourself in every challenge, every transition, and every state of your nervous system.

You have spent your time with this book learning to inhabit your body with more gentleness, clarity, and truth. You have explored the stories that shaped you, discovered the wounds that needed tending, and learned how to anchor your nervous system into safety. You have remembered who you are beneath survival mode. You have rebuilt your connection to your inner compass, and practiced visibility, boundaries, presence, contentment, gratitude, rooted worthiness, and aligned creation.

Integration asks you to carry these lessons forward, not perfectly, but consistently. You will still have days where the inner critic is loud. You may slip into old patterns or feel the familiar pull of people-pleasing, urgency, comparison, or overwhelm. But now, you know how to find your way back.

You have the tools. You have the awareness. You have the somatic language of safety inside you. Healing does not mean that you will never get dysregulated again; it means knowing how to return home to yourself when you drift.

Pillars of Nervous System Wealth (Integration Framework)

Daily Regulation Practices

Your nervous system is foundational in your life. Small, daily practices such as breathwork, grounding, slowing down, and mindful presence keep the foundation steady. These moments compound over time.

Boundaries as Self-Respect

Boundaries are how you protect your peace and your energy. Holding them is not selfish; it's an act of worthiness.

Presence as a Way of Seeing the World

Presence allows you to experience life as it unfolds, rather than through the lens of fear or the pull of old narratives.

Choosing Alignment over Approval

Authenticity strengthens self-trust. Every time you choose your truth instead of performing for acceptance, your nervous system learns that your truth is safe.

Honoring Your Capacity & Receiving Rhythm

Rest is not a reward; it is a requirement. When you honor your capacity, you create a sustainable path that allows growth to happen without collapse or burnout.

Designing Forward with Intention

You are no longer moving through life on autopilot. You are designing your days, your actions, your relationships, and your future from a place of worth and aligned with your values.

Walking the Path You Have Built

You've reached the final chapter, but this is not an ending. Take a moment to recognize the ground you have walked, the patterns you have shed, the roots you have grown, and the inner safety you have reclaimed.

The teachings in this book are not isolated ideas; they are an intentional sequence, one chapter building on the next. When viewed together, they form a nervous system supported map for living a life anchored in self-worth, clarity, and expansion.

Let's look at each chapter one more time to weave everything together, step by step, so you can feel the fullness of your own transformation.

Root: Reclaiming Safety & Self-Compassion

You learned to remember yourself.

Chapter 1: The Myth of Brokenness

You began by learning that you were never broken. You were responding exactly as a human nervous system responds to overwhelm, stress, or trauma. What you felt was not failure, but adaptation. This truth alone softened shame and created the foundation for change.

Chapter 2: Nervous System 101: Your Inner Compass

You learned how your nervous system communicates safety and threat, how regulation feels in the body, and how dysregulation hijacks perception. You met states and cues, and you finally had language for sensations you have carried for years.

Chapter 3: Conditioning, Inherited Beliefs & Generational Healing

You explored the beliefs you inherited: narratives about worth, work, identity, money, emotion, and safety. You learned that many of your patterns did not begin with you; they were inherited survival strategies. Awareness became a chance for liberation.

Chapter 4: The Disconnect Between Safety & Success

Here you discovered why "wanting more" often activates fear. You came to understand why ambition triggers anxiety when your nervous system has not yet associated expansion with safety. You learned that abundance cannot be forced from a dysregulated body. It must be allowed from a deep sense of safety.

Chapter 5: Safety as the Soil of Creative Growth

You learned to soften your inner landscape, create body-based safety cues, and reconnect to sensation. This chapter taught you that your creativity, intuition, and clarity thrive only in soil that feels safe.

Chapter 6: Shadow Work & Emotional Integration

You met the parts of yourself you once avoided: anger, jealousy, fear, neediness, perfectionism, defensiveness. Instead of rejecting them, you learned to listen. You recognized that their purpose was protection.

Chapter 7: Recognizing Triggers, Patterns & Emotions

Awareness became embodiment. You learned to observe rather than collapse, pause rather than react, name rather than numb. You mapped your patterns and felt your emotional waves with compassion, not self-judgment.

Chapter 8: The Somatic Language of Forgiveness

Forgiveness became a nervous system process for your own healing rather than a moral obligation. You learned to release emotional residues, not to excuse what happened, but to free your body from holding it.

Rise: Building from Safety into Self-Trust

You learned to respond differently.

Chapter 9: Rewriting Your Story

You confronted the internal narratives and stories that shaped your identity. You began choosing new meanings, new language, and new interpretations aligned with truth rather than fear.

Chapter 10: Emotional Repatterning & Inner Dialogue

You learned to become the observer of your inner world with curiosity and compassion, to talk to yourself with respect, and to guide your emotions instead of being consumed by them.

Chapter 11: Healing the Inner Critic & Self-Respect Wounds

You learned to soften the old voice that once kept you small. You stopped abandoning yourself and learned that self-respect is built through small, aligned choices. You also learned that your nervous system blooms under kindness.

Chapter 12: Boundaries as a Nervous System Practice

You learned to create safety internally and externally. Boundaries became a form of self-trust. You also learned that boundaries regulate your nervous system more effectively than willpower alone.

Chapter 13: Designing from Rooted Worthiness

You shifted from forcing to listening and from urgency to alignment. You learned to plan from embodied decision-making, not hustle and pressure.

Chapter 14: Not Reacting to Drama: The Power of Peace

You learned to opt out of chaos, to refuse emotional reactivity as a lifestyle, and to protect your inner peace instead of trying to manage external storms.

Chapter 15: Protecting Your Energy & Staying Resourced

You learned how to notice drains, nourish your system, and rebuild your internal reserves. You stopped leaking energy into people-pleasing, over-functioning, or emotional labor that wasn't yours.

Chapter 16: Happiness, Presence, Gratitude & Nervous System Wealth

You discovered that contentment is the bridge to joy. You learned this sequence: contentment, mindfulness, presence, gratitude, and joy. You also practiced creating micro-moments of regulation that expand your sense of embodied worthiness.

Design: Creating Your Life from Embodied Worthiness

You learned to build a life that matches your nervous system, values, and truth.

Chapter 17: Rooted Visibility, Authentic Expression & Soul-Aligned Success

You reclaimed your voice. You learned about the visibility window, the cost of self-silencing, and the somatic signature of authenticity. You practiced speaking truth without abandoning yourself and began expanding into aligned success.

Chapter 18: Creating a Worthy Life

You learned to create from sufficiency rather than urgency, and from alignment rather than pressure. You explored capacity-based design, values-based decisions, and habits that support your long-term worthiness.

Chapter 19: The Wealth of Being You

You stopped placing your worth in what you produce. You learned to care for the vessel: your mind, body, and energy. You redefined success through alignment, not exhaustion, and discovered that nervous system wealth begins from within.

Chapter 20: Designing Forward

You became the creator of your life. You practiced personal responsibility, energetic alignment, and pace-based expansion. You learned how to build habits that support your vision and how to trust the path before you.

Chapter 21: Integration: Living the Work

You learned that nervous system wealth is not a destination that you arrive at, but that it is a lifelong journey that you weave into your daily life. You have arrived here, not as the person you were when you began, but as someone who has met yourself more deeply, more honestly, and more compassionately.

Integration as an Ongoing Journey

Although you have reached the end of this book, you have not reached the end of your healing. Nervous system wealth is a way of life. Integration is the bridge between the inner work you have done and the outer life you're creating. It is the ongoing commitment to tend to your nervous system, practice self-respect, choose aligned action, and root into contentment, presence, and embodied worthiness.

You have learned to regulate your nervous system, rewrite old narratives, speak your truth, honor your capacity, design from alignment, and walk forward with clarity, presence, and a deep sense of self-respect. Every chapter built toward the same truth: You were never broken. You were always worthy. You can move forward in your embodied life with reverence and gratitude.

Trust that you will continue to both expand and deepen your relationship with yourself. Trust that you will know when you need rest and when you are ready to grow. Trust that the truest version of you is now leading the way. You are the writer of your own story.

Healing is not a straight line, and you can revisit these chapters again and again, each time from a deeper, more resourced version of yourself. That is not regression; it is courageous growth.

A Final Blessing for Your Path Forward

May you trust the wisdom of your body.

May you honor the pace of your nervous system.

May you remember your inherent worth.

May you choose alignment over approval.

May you continue to design your life from a place of truth, safety, and soul alignment.

You no longer have to search for your worth.

It has always lived within you.

Root into yourself. Rise into your life. Spread your wings and soar.

You deserve everything you desire and more because you are bravely, fiercely, and unapologetically you.

Nervous System Reset: Restoring Ease & Expanding Capacity

Nervous System Resets are a way of returning to yourself through gentle, supportive habits that build resilience over time. They restore ease, expand your capacity, and reconnect you with your body in ways that feel nourishing.

You may move between these pathways throughout your life, your seasons, or even within the same week. There is no finish line here, and there are no levels to master or graduate into. They are invitations you respond to based on your capacity, energy, and circumstances. Some days, restoration is the most regulated choice. Other days, gentle expansion feels available. Both are expressions of nervous system wealth.

Restoring Ease & Comfort

These practices help shift your body from subtle stress into a state of ease and replenishment:

- Add more nourishing, colorful, whole foods in ways that feel supportive and satisfying.

- Watch a funny show or movie to bring more laughter into your day.

- Use a foam roller or roll a tennis ball under your feet to release tension.

- Take a warm bath with essential oils, candles, or Epsom salts to support relaxation.

- Try a new kind of gentle movement. Have you been curious about yoga, tai chi, or qigong? Try a beginner video online and follow along.

- Read a book purely for pleasure or inspiration.
- Dance while brushing your teeth.

Expansion, Joy & Reconnection

These practices help you expand your window of capacity, discover joy, and step into a more resourced state:

- Try a new hobby to bring fresh curiosity and joy into your life.
- Volunteer or join a club to build connections with others, find purpose, and build community.
- Sign up for a class to explore something new that excites you.
- Buy yourself flowers. It's a simple act of self-kindness.
- Schedule a massage, facial, or restorative treatment.

These pathways are not about productivity or self-improvement. They are about allowing your nervous system to experience safe visibility, connection, and joy beyond your inner world. These resets strengthen your nervous system by building consistent cues of safety, joy, and nourishment. When you honor what fuels you, physically, emotionally, and energetically, your entire life begins to feel more peaceful and grounded.

Advanced Integration: The Spa Day at Home Ritual

We often postpone rest or self-care until things slow down, or maybe when we do have a few minutes to relax, we don't feel like putting forth the effort for self-care, but our nervous system learns from what we repeatedly do, not what we intend to do. A simple, intentional spa-like ritual teaches your body that rest, pleasure, softness, and comfort are safe to receive. This practice is about retraining your system to associate relaxation with safety rather than guilt.

The Practice

1. Prepare your space. Dim the lights. Light candles (safely). Turn on soothing music or nature sounds. Add an essential oil diffuser if you like. Wrap yourself in a soft robe or blanket.

2. Choose your water ritual. Either soak your feet in warm water or run a bath. Add Epsom salts or magnesium flakes. Add a few drops of essential oils and scatter dried flower petals if you want an elevated experience.

3. Soothe and soften. Use a gentle salt or sugar scrub. Massage it slowly into your arms, legs, or shoulders. Let yourself feel the sensation of tension dissolving. Try a peppermint foot rub. Use a moisturizing body oil, or apply a face mask. Let each step be done with tenderness, not urgency.

4. Support your senses. Sip herbal tea, lemon water, or sparkling water. Place cool cucumber slices over your eyes. Let your breath slow naturally.

This ritual is a form of integration. Every moment you allow your body to soften, you are sending a powerful message: *Rest is safe. Pleasure is allowed. Comfort is nourishment.*

The more your nervous system experiences these states, the more accessible they become, and the more your body learns to receive.

Journal Prompts

Notice

- Are there sections of this book that resonated strongly with you? Were there parts that didn't resonate, or that brought up resistance? What might those reactions be trying to show you?

- Did any chapter trigger a strong emotional response? What did that response feel like in your body, and what might it reveal about areas still needing tenderness or healing?

- What have you learned about your nervous system's cues, boundaries, and capacity? Can you name at least one way you relate to yourself differently now?

Reflect

- Reflect on who you were when you first opened this book. How did you feel in your body? What did you believe about yourself back then? What has shifted?

- Which chapter or concept do you feel most excited to return to again as you continue your healing?

Integrate

- Are there practices you want to commit to carrying forward? Which feel the most grounding, accessible, or transformative?

- When you imagine continuing this work six months from now, what feels most important to protect: your energy, your boundaries, your rest, or your sense of self? What might help you stay connected to that?

- What would you like to thank your past self for? What would you like to promise your future self?

Rewiring Your Outlook

I am worthy by design.

QUICK REFERENCE GUIDE

The Three Primary Nervous System States

Regulated / Ventral Vagal (Safety & Connection)
You feel grounded, present, steady, open, creative.

Body cues: steady breath, soft shoulders, clear thinking

Accessed through: presence, grounding, micro-moments of joy, deep rest, connection

Sympathetic Activation (Fight / Flight)
You feel urgent, pressured, activated, overwhelmed.

Body cues: racing thoughts, tight chest, clenched jaw, shallow breath

Triggers: stress, deadlines, conflict, overcommitment

Soothed by: movement, intentional breathing, boundaries, slowing pace

Dorsal Vagal (Freeze / Shutdown)
You feel depleted, numb, shut down, disconnected, unmotivated.

Body cues: heaviness, foggy thinking, cold hands, collapse in posture

Triggers: chronic stress, overstimulation, burnout, emotional overload

Soothed by: warmth, gentle movement, micro pleasure, sensory input, compassion

Signs Your Nervous System Is Coming Back to Regulation

- You sigh naturally.
- Your shoulders drop.
- Your breath deepens.
- Your chest feels warm or open.
- Your thoughts become clearer.
- You feel more capable and less reactive.
- You return to curiosity.

Reset Your Nervous System in Just a Few Minutes

You've likely seen many of these suggestions before. Most are simple, accessible, and take only a few minutes. Yet the hardest part is rarely *doing* them, rather it is giving ourselves permission to pause, to care for ourselves, and to meet our bodies with compassion instead of criticism. Sometimes we hide or downplay our self-care rituals because we fear judgment from others or feel guilty prioritizing ourselves. But remember, nervous system regulation is not indulgent; it is foundational. These micro resets give your body the evidence it needs to feel safe, grounded, and supported.

Breath-Based Resets

Box breathing: Inhale for four. Hold for four. Exhale for four. Hold for four. Then repeat.

4–7–8 breath: Inhale for four. Hold for seven. Exhale for eight.

Alternate nostril breathing: Inhale through one nostril while closing the other. Then switch and exhale though the opposite side, alternating with each breath.

Long exhale breathing: Exhale for twice as long as you inhale.

Breath of gratitude: Inhale "thank." Exhale "you."

Sensory Grounding Resets

Try 5–4–3–2–1 grounding: five things you see, four things you feel, three things you hear, two things you smell, one thing you taste.

Hold something warm, like a mug of tea in both hands.

Squeeze a stress ball.

Listen to calming or instrumental music.

Look at something beautiful in nature (even a photo).

Light a candle and watch the flame.

Wrap yourself in a soft blanket.

Movement & Posture Resets

Try gentle neck circles.

Roll your shoulders forward and backward.

Bounce lightly on your toes.

Shake out your arms and legs.

Stretch your spine (e.g., side bends, forward roll).

Walk for a couple of minutes.

Press your feet firmly into the floor and spread your toes.

Do a slow cat-cow movement.

Self-Soothing Resets

Try a gentle face massage.

Place your hand over your heart.

Use a weighted blanket.

Mindful Observation Resets

Watch clouds move across the sky.

Smell something that you love.

Watch a candle flame.

Observe shadows and light in the room.

Follow a single sound until it fades.

Mini Meditation Resets

Repeat a calming mantra like *I am safe in this moment*, or *Nothing is required of me this second*.

Visualize a peaceful place.

Tune in to one full inhale and exhale.

Sit in silence for one minute.

Imagine a warm light surrounding your body.

Vagus Nerve Stimulation Resets

Gargle water.

Hum your favorite song.

Splash cool water on your face.

Laugh!

Sing out loud.

Quick Nature Connection Resets

Step outside for fresh air.

Feel sunlight on your face.

Stand barefoot on the grass.

Listen to birds.

Feel the breeze on your skin.

Hold a leaf or stone.

Notice the temperature of the air on your skin.

Gratitude Resets

Name one thing you're grateful for.

Recall a positive memory.

Think of someone you love.

Thank your body for something it does for you.

Offer appreciation for something small and ordinary.

Money Blocks & Reframes

"We're not the kind of people who have money."

"You have to sacrifice yourself to succeed."

"If you earn more than the rest of your family, you'll be judged or abandoned."

"Stay humble and don't outshine anyone."

"Success requires constant hustle."

"Keep yourself busy."

"Rest is laziness."

"Success means having more, not being more."

"If I make more money, people will expect more from me."

"People will only love me for what I provide."

"My worth is tied to my usefulness."

"It's more noble to struggle."

"It's safer to stay small."

"Receiving is uncomfortable; giving is safer."

"More money = more pressure."

Block: "I'll become too much for people if I grow."

Reframe: "The people meant for me expand with me. Authentic relationships welcome my growth."

Block: "Success will make me visible, and visibility isn't safe."

Reframe: "I can expand at a pace that feels safe to my body."

Block: "If I have more, I'll lose it."

Reframe: "I can build capacity gently. I am allowed to hold more without fear."

Block: "If I become successful, I'll lose touch with myself."

Reframe: "Success built from my values and integrity deepens my authenticity instead of threatening it."

Block: "Wanting money makes me greedy."

Reframe: "Resourcing myself allows me to flourish. And when I flourish, I have more capacity to help others."

Block: "More money means more responsibility, and I can't handle that stress."

Reframe: "I can expand in ways that honor my nervous system and capacity. Expansion does not require burnout."

Block: "People like us don't make money."

Reframe: "My lineage does not limit my future. I can honor where I come from and still choose a new path."

Rituals of Reconnection & Creative Alchemy Toolbox

Rituals of reconnection are gentle, embodied practices that remind the nervous system that safety can be created through intention, presence, and repetition. When you treat ordinary moments as sacred, you turn everyday life into a ceremony of self-worth.

You can use the principle of habit stacking to anchor these micro rituals into your day by attaching it to something you are already doing, such as waking up, making coffee, or brushing your teeth. You can create rituals of reconnection in daily, weekly, and monthly cycles, or perhaps even tied to the lunar or seasonal cycles. You can also choose intentional pauses in between projects.

As you find different practices that help sustain your inner capacity, consider the following types of nourishment:

- Physical nourishment: gentle movement, rest, grounding practices
- Emotional nourishment: connection, laughter, boundaries, self-expression
- Spiritual nourishment: reflection, nature, creativity, beauty
- Nervous system nourishment: slowness, presence, breath, quiet

Morning Rituals

Place a hand on your heart. Take three slow breaths, and name one thing you appreciate.

Sip your morning tea or coffee slowly while noticing the aroma, warmth, and flavor.

Read one page from an inspirational book.

Do a sixty-second stretch before looking at your phone.

Open a window for fresh air, and take three grounding breaths.

Evening Rituals

Dim the lights and play soft music.

Do a gentle face massage while thanking your skin.

Reflect on one moment of the day that made you feel proud.

Turn down your bed with intention.

Light a candle and write in your gratitude journal.

Weekly Reset Rituals

Take an Epsom salt bath.

Go for a nature walk or hike.

Declutter one drawer or corner.

Review your week with compassion and aligned with capacity.

Monthly, Seasonal, or Lunar Cycle Rituals

Declutter or rearrange a room or section of the house.

Set a fresh intention for the new month, new season, or new moon cycle.

Update your vision board.

Create something with natural materials.

Have a reset evening with candles, tea, and reflection.

Creative Alchemy Toolbox

These are tiny creative practices that move energy, shift mood, and reconnect you with curiosity and play.

Write three sentences of stream of consciousness.

Press a leaf or flower in a notebook.

Make a small arrangement with objects that symbolize your values.

Do a two-minute doodle.

Collect inspiring colors, textures, or images.

Rearrange a bookshelf or create a small vignette.

Write a short poem.

Make something beautiful out of something ordinary.

Integration Summary

Each stage of your three-part journey—Root, Rise, and Design—helps you heal your nervous system, reclaim your worth, and create a life aligned with who you truly are. Use this reference guide whenever you need a quick way to reconnect to the path.

Root: Reclaiming Safety & Self-Compassion

You began by remembering that nothing about you is broken. Your nervous system was simply adapting and protecting you. The Root phase taught you safety, awareness, and softness—the foundation for all future growth. In this section, you learned to:

- Understand your nervous system and its states
- Recognize conditioning, generational beliefs, and inherited patterns
- Explore the disconnect between safety and success
- Reconnect with your body as a safe home
- Meet your shadow with compassion
- Identify triggers, emotional patterns, and somatic cues
- Release emotional residue through forgiveness

Rise: Building from Safety into Self-Trust

Here, you shifted from survival-driven habits to soul-aligned choices. The Rise phase reconnected you to your voice, your capacity, and your inner leadership. You learned to:

- Rewrite the stories that shaped your identity
- Reshape your inner dialogue and emotional patterns

- Heal the inner critic and rebuild self-respect
- Use boundaries as a nervous system practice
- Design your life from the body, not from pressure
- Step out of reactivity and into peace
- Protect your energy and stay resourced
- Cultivate presence and gratitude as daily nervous system wealth

Design: Creating Your Life from Embodied Worthiness

You stepped into creation, not from urgency or proving, but from grounded self-worth. The Design phase taught you how to build a life that your nervous system can safely and sustainably hold. You learned to:

- Practice rooted visibility and authentic expression
- Create from sufficiency rather than lack
- Align your goals with values, boundaries, and capacity
- Care for the vessel (your energy, body, and truth)
- Redefine success by alignment, not output
- Design forward with intention, responsibility, and clarity
- Build habits and rhythms that support your future self

Across all three phases, you learned to:

- Honor your body as your compass
- Soothe your nervous system and create internal safety
- Shift from scarcity to sufficiency
- Choose alignment over approval
- Trust your inner wisdom
- Root into your inherent worthiness

This journey was never about becoming someone new, but about remembering who you are.

May you root deeply.

May you rise steadily.

May you design with intention and self-trust.

ENDNOTES

Sources are referenced to acknowledge foundational influences rather than to serve as academic citations.

Stephen W. Porges — understanding how the nervous system responds to safety, threat, and connection

Deb Dana — practical, nervous-system-informed approaches to regulation and resilience

Bessel van der Kolk — how trauma is held in the body and nervous system

Peter A. Levine — restoring safety and regulation after stress and trauma

Pat Ogden — body-based approaches to emotional awareness and healing

Carl Jung — the role of the unconscious and shadow aspects of the self

Kristin Neff — the impact of self-compassion on emotional well-being

Daniel J. Siegel — how the brain, body, and relationships shape emotional health

Rick Hanson – how repeated experiences shape emotional patterns and inner resilience

Everett Worthington – forgiveness as a process of emotional and psychological healing

Morrnah Nalamaku Simeona – reconciliation and self-forgiveness practices adapted from hoʻoponopono

ACKNOWLEDGEMENTS

To my editor Jenna Nelson. Thank you for your careful attention and steady refinement of these pages. Your precision strengthened both the structure and coherence of this work. Your ability to see what the book already was, and gently guide it into form, made all the difference. I am deeply grateful for your support and guidance throughout this process.

To my proofreader Trinity McFadden. Thank you for your attention to detail and for bringing a final layer of polish to these pages.

To my designer Ian Koviak. Thank you for bringing visual clarity and calm to this work. Your design created spaciousness and cohesion, allowing the writing to breathe. The reader's journey through these pages is shaped by your thoughtful artistry.

To the teachers, practitioners, and writers whose work on nervous system healing shaped the field long before this book existed.

To my husband, who read early drafts and offered steady encouragement throughout this process. Thank you for your steadiness, patience, and belief. Your support made this work possible.

To my children, whose presence continually reminds me why this work matters. This journey has been shaped by you more than you know.

To the readers who find themselves here. Thank you for your willingness to slow down, listen inward, and choose a more rooted way of living.

ABOUT THE AUTHOR

Janet Brown is a writer focused on nervous system literacy, embodied self-worth, and sustainable expansion. Weaving together gentle awareness and reflective inquiry, she explores how safety within the body shapes the lives we build. Her work draws from personal study, lived experience, and the deep belief that lasting change begins with internal safety.

Continue the Journey
Worthy by Design introduces a broader body of work devoted to nervous system wealth and grounded life design. This book is meant to serve as a foundation—a place to return to as you build safety, clarity, and self-trust.

To continue the work beyond these pages, visit:
nswealthstudio.com

Ongoing writing and reflections are available at:
nervoussystemwealth.substack.com